# Designer Beadwork
## French Beaded Designs

# Designer Beadwork
## French Beaded Designs

*Donna DeAngelis Dickt*

**Sterling Publishing Co., Inc. New York**
A Sterling/Chapelle Book

Chapelle, Ltd.
Jo Packham • Sara Toliver • Cindy Stoeckl • Matt DaMaio

*Editor:* Karmen Quinney

*Book Design:* Rose Sheifer

*Photostylist:* Rebecca Ittner

*Photographer:* Vince Lupo


Library of Congress Cataloging-in-Publication Data

Dickt, Donna DeAngelis.
Designer beadwork: French beaded designs/Donna DeAngelis Dickt.
   p.cm.
Includes index.
ISBN 1-4027-1603-6
1. Bead flowers. I. Title.

TT890.2.D53 2005
745.58'2--dc22           2004020101

10 9 8 7 6 5 4 3 2 1

Published by Sterling Publishing Co., Inc.
387 Park Avenue South, New York, NY 10016
©2005 by Donna DeAngelis Dickt
Distributed in Canada by Sterling Publishing
c/o Manda Group, 165 Dufferin Street
Toronto, Ontario, Canada M6K 3H6
Distributed in Great Britain by Chrysalis Books Group PLC, The
Chrysalis Building, Bramley Road, London W10 6SP, England
Distributed in Australia by Capricorn Link (Australia) Pty. Ltd.
P.O. Box 704, Windsor, NSW 2756, Australia
Printed in China
All Rights Reserved

Sterling ISBN 1-4027-1603-6

Write Us

If you have questions or comments, please contact:
   Chapelle, Ltd., Inc.,
   P.O. Box 9252, Ogden, UT 84409
   (801) 621-2777 • (801) 621-2788 Fax
   e-mail: chapelle@chapelleltd.com
   Web site: chapelleltd.com


A special thank-you to the following for allowing us to photograph parts of this book in their businesses. Their trust and
cooperation are greatly appreciated.

The Grapevine—Home and Garden Accessories
117 E. Patrick St.
Fredrick, MD 21701
(301) 663-3920

McCleery's Flat Bed and Breakfast
121 E. Patrick St.
Fredrick, MD 21701
(800) 774-7926

# TABLE OF CONTENTS

# INTRODUCTION

Open the pages of any home decor magazine and it would be almost impossible not to see the handiwork of a floral designer. From the simplicity of a single-stem bud vase to the grandness of a center hall arrangement, flowers have been a source of decorative accent in the home for centuries. Over the years trends have come and gone, and styles have changed, but the use of flowers as a decorative accessory still prevails.

As a bead artist, I found myself drawn to the history and tradition of creating floral designs with beads. Although very little has been documented about the history of French beaded flowers, it is believed to be a centuries-old craft that originated in either France or Italy. French beading refers to the technique of wrapping beads, strung on wire, to create beautiful flowers. Although originally intended as church adornments and memorials, beaded flowers were eventually brought into the home as decorative accents. It was during the Victorian era that the use of beaded flowers in home decor became more prevalent.

I have been teaching the traditions of French beaded flowers for six years. I learned the techniques from my grandmother at a young age. But like many young children, I saw it as something fun to do for a while and soon moved on to other childhood activities. When I returned to the craft many years later, it all came back to me. I haven't stopped beading since!

In all the years that I have been beading flowers, it never ceases to amaze me how fascinated people of all ages are with the sparkle and color of tiny beads. I often bring my beadwork with me when I travel or while I am waiting for my children's music lessons or sports practices to finish. I have been spotted beading in the car pool line and in the doctor's waiting room. People are drawn to the beads and want to know what I am doing. When I show them a petal or leaf, or the wing of a butterfly, they want to know more. They ask how and, of course, I am all too willing to demonstrate. In a short period of time their amazement grows with the realization that it is not really all that difficult.

Vintage Memorial Wreath

Detail of *Vintage Memorial Wreath*

*Poppies and Anemones*, c. 1970, made by my Grandmother.

In all the years in which I have been beading flowers, it never ceases to amaze me how fascinated people of all ages are with the sparkle and color of tiny beads.

And, wow, how beautiful! A flower, a butterfly, a tree; but what do you do with it?

What do you do with it? It is the million-dollar question. It is the question that I am most often asked, even by students who have been beading with me for years. Sometimes I find myself simply staring back with what I am certain is a blank look on my face. After all, isn't it beautiful just to look at and admire? But then I realize, for many, function over form will always be at the heart of their craft.

So with that in mind, I have set out to show you how easily you can transform the beauty of a beaded flower into a functioning accessory for your home. And with a little practice and imagination, you will be able to create your own designs, using the basic techniques of French beaded flowers. However, I must warn you, you will never be able to open the pages of a home decor magazine again without thinking "I can bead that."

*Sugarplum Fairy Tree*, c. 1970, made by my Grandmother.

## How to Use This Book

If you have never made a beaded flower before, you may look at the projects in this book and think they are beyond your abilities. Nothing could be further from the truth! Once you have learned a few simple techniques, you will be very surprised to find that many of the projects that appear to be overwhelming, and look difficult at first glance, are in fact simple and straightforward, and can be easily accomplished with a little practice.

The purpose of this book is to provide everyone, from the complete novice to the most advanced beader, with the appropriate instruction for the techniques needed to accomplish a wide range of projects that will satisfy many different skill levels. If you have never beaded before, I recommend that you begin at the beginning. The section on Beading Basics on pages 9–14 will familiarize you with the tools, beads, wire, and other supplies that are necessary to create the beautiful projects on the following pages. The Glossary on pages 123–124 will also be a helpful guide for all skill levels.

The first half of the book is designed to teach you the techniques of French beaded flowers by making several different individual flowers. The skills needed to create each new flower build upon the techniques presented in the instructions for the previous flower. Therefore, I recommend that you learn each flower in the order that I have presented them. Of course, you may be anxious to try some of the projects presented in the second half of the book before working your way through all the flowers. I actually encourage this. So that you don't get frustrated by attempting something you haven't yet learned, I have made suggestions after each of the individual flowers as to those projects that can be successfully attempted before moving on to the next flower. It will give you greater enjoyment, and more practice, before you move on to the more advanced flowers. You will be amazed how quickly you can progress if you keep to the succession of the book.

If you have some experience with beaded flowers and you want to jump around and try different things, you can refer to the section in each of the instructions which identifies the techniques that you should know in order to be able to complete the flower or project. Under the header "What You Need to Know," you will find a list of the techniques that will not be demonstrated in that particular flower or project. You will be expected to know that technique. Under the header "What You Will Learn," you will find a list of the techniques that will be demonstrated and fully described within those instructions. This should help you quickly pinpoint and identify the exact skill level of a particular flower or project. If something looks unfamiliar to you, simply refer to the page indicated for that technique. Remember that the flowers are presented in the order that the techniques are introduced and they build upon each other.

The last half of the book includes several projects that use the flowers, which were taught in the first part of the book. Some projects use the exact flower patterns found in the book, and others use variations of those flowers. Whenever I have used variations of a flower pattern, I have included specific instructions for achieving that variation. If the pattern is exactly the same, I have simply referred you to the directions in the first half of the book.

I hope you will find the projects to be inspirational, and that they will motivate you to create your own designs. Most of all have fun with the flowers and the projects, whether you are learning this beautiful craft for the first time or returning to it after many years.

Top row from left to right: loose by the bag; on strings, by the half-kilo; lose by tube. Bottom row from left to right: loose by the bag; individual hank; loose by the bag.

# Beading Basics

Before you get started, it would be helpful to familiarize yourself with the tools and supplies that you will be using. Over the years, I have become partial to certain brands and types of supplies, especially wire and tools. I recognize that there is a wide choice in the market and I will make every effort to describe your options while noting why I have chosen a particular wire or tool as my preference. Often, cost will be a factor as you decide between two or more options. I will also try to suggest when I think it is OK to choose the least expensive option and when I think the extra money spent for a more expensive option is well worth it, and why.

## BEADS

Let's begin by taking a look at the different types of beads that are available to you. In general, I make my flowers with one of two sizes of seed beads. I have designed the flowers and projects in this book for size 11° seed beads or size 9° three-cuts. If you fall in love with another size bead and would like to try it, by all means do. Please note, however, that the quantity of beads that are shown in the patterns may change slightly as you change the size of the bead. Also, the final appearance of the flower may change slightly as you move up or down in bead size. The higher the number of the bead, the smaller the bead size. If you like the look of the smaller beads you may also need to adjust the wire size to accommodate a smaller hole size. Some flowers such as the tulips and anemones will not hold up well with a thinner wire, especially the tulip leaves, which are very long and wide.

Size 11° seed beads are usually rounder, smoother beads. There may be a slight variation in the size of each bead, depending on where the beads were made. In general, beads from the Czech Republic are not quite as uniform in size and shape as beads from Japan. This is not necessarily a bad thing. I actually prefer the variation of the Czech beads and the naturalness of the results produced by the irregular size and shape. That is not to say that I do not use Japanese beads. Sometimes I find a color in a Japanese bead that I just have to have, and so I don't worry so much about the uniformity of the beads.

Size 9° three-cut beads are my favorite. They are approximately the same size as an 11° seed bead; but instead of being smooth, each bead has three cuts down the sides of the bead. These cuts make the beads sparkle. They tend to be very rough on the edges and make for less-smooth curves, but the sparkle makes the flower magnificent. Because of the roughness around small curves, I tend not to use them when a flower calls for wrapped, beaded stems. For this, I will use the rounder size 11° seed bead. To get the best of both looks, mix the two types of beads in the same flower, using the three-cut beads for the petals and centers, and the size 11° seed beads for the stems and leaves. The disadvantage of using size 9° three-cut beads is the cost. They are much more expensive than the size 11° seed beads. However, I enjoy the sparkle in the flower so much that I sacrifice the extra cost. To me, it is definitely worth it.

Beads can be purchased in a couple different ways. Seed beads are available loose, by the bag; loose, by the tube; on strings, by the individual hank; or on hanks, by the half kilo. The most economical way to purchase beads is on hanks, by the half-kilo bag. A half kilo of size 11° seed beads contains 12 hanks, where each hank contains 12 strands that are approximately 19"–20" long. Size 9° three-cut beads can be purchased by the bag, called a bunch. Each bunch contains 10 hanks, where each hank contains 10 strands that are approximately 17"–18" long.

Because there are fewer beads in a hank of size 9° three-cuts than in a hank of size 11° seed beads, I have compensated for this in the instructions. If the instructions call for one hank, you may use either size bead and still have enough beads to complete the project. Often you will have more than enough beads. The quantities of materials in the instructions allow you to make one flower.

To equate the quantities of loose beads to the hank measurements, estimate that one hank of size 11° seed beads equals approximately 47 grams. Loose beads are often packaged in 20-gram tubes, so you would need approximately 2½ tubes to make one hank.

As far as colors and finishes of beads are concerned, the choice is entirely up to you. Color is the one element of design that can be extremely personal. Bead colors used in each project have been listed in the project's material list. However, I encourage you to experiment with different colors and determine for yourself what suits your own taste. When choosing colors, give consideration to where the finished item will be placed in your home, and coordinate the bead colors with your home decor color scheme.

## WIRE

Wire is the second most important element in making French beaded flowers. While it is true that the beads cover most of the wire, and it is often our goal to make the wire as invisible as possible, please do not dismiss the wire as being incidental to the beauty of the flower. It is the wire that gives structure to your flowers and will ultimately ensure that your flowers last a lifetime.

There are many types of wire on the market, ranging in quality from inexpensive craft wire to more-expensive colored copper wire. These two types of wire are sold on spools or on paddles. Each type is suitable for different purposes in flower beading. A third type of wire needed to make flowers is florists' stem wire. These wires are thicker and heavier, and are sold in straight lengths bundled in packages.

When creating the petals, centers, or leaves of a flower, I prefer to use colored copper wire. Unlike many craft wires, which are often painted steel, colored copper wire is permanently colored. The color on painted wire tends to crack and even rub off at times. Cracks in the paint will increase the rate of oxidation of the wire and over time will accelerate the deterioration of the flower. Colored copper wire is a little more expensive. However, I like knowing that all the time I have invested in making the flowers will pay off in the future with flowers that will last.

Top row from left to right: 5 spools of colored copper wire; spool of 30-gauge green paddle wire. Bottom row from left to right: 3 spools of assembly wire; stem wire in 16- and 18-gauge.

Copper wire tends to be a softer wire than steel wire, so it facilitates making smoother curves and more delicate loops. The stiffness of craft wire makes it more suitable to the assembly aspect of flower beading. I recommend craft wire or florists' "paddle" wire when putting the flowers together. Paddle wire is simply green or silver craft wire wrapped on paddles. It is very inexpensive and works great for the assembly.

The third type of wire, florists' stem wire, is the wire that you will use for the stems of your flowers. It is sometimes sold with a thread covering over the wire. I prefer to use wire with no extra covering. The thread on some wire will add another thickness to your stem, but will not offer any additional strength. When assembling the flower, you will want to keep the stems as thin as possible and still be able to support all the petals and leaves.

All wire, regardless of what it is made from, is measured in gauges that correspond to the thickness of the

wire. For most flowers in this book you will need 24-, 26-, or 28-gauge wire to create the petals, centers, and leaves. The higher the number, the thinner the wire is. To lace, or tie, the rows together, 30- or 32-gauge wire is necessary. The thinness of this wire will allow it to almost disappear between the beads while still doing the job of holding the rows together.

Stem wire can be found in 16- or 18-gauge pieces. These are generally sold in 18" lengths. Sometimes two or three pieces will be needed to hold a heavy flower. I will also show you how to create a longer stem utilizing several pieces of both gauges of wire.

To attach the petals, centers, and leaves to the stem wire, use 30-gauge, green, paddle wire. You may also use any 28-gauge assembly wire made of steel for the assembly. The 28-gauge steel wire is sturdier than 28-gauge copper wire. Avoid using 28-gauge copper wire to assemble.

From left to right, on top of a bead mat: mahogany bead spinner with wire-twisting device; nylon-jaw pliers; round-nosed pliers; ruler; and craft scissors. On the right side of bead mat, from top to bottom: large-wire cutters; oak bead spinner; small-wire cutters.

## GENERAL TOOLS

Keep your toolbox simple. You will need the following tools to make all of the flowers and projects in this book:

- Bead mat—to catch any beads that may spill as you work.
- Bead spinner—to facilitate stringing the beads onto the wire.
- Craft scissors—to cut the beads off the hank and to cut the floral tape.
- Heavy-duty wire cutters—for cutting the heavier gauge stem wires.
- Nylon-jaw pliers—to take out any kinks in your wire.
- Round-nosed pliers—for making very small loops and tight bends in the wire.
- Ruler that denotes 1/8'' intervals—to measure beads or length of wire as you create the flower parts.
- Small wire cutters—for cutting the wire that you use to make your petals, centers, and leaves.

Let me take a moment to address the second item, a bead spinner. When I first started making beaded flowers, I didn't use a bead spinner. I simply strung the beads onto the wire by hand directly off the hank, the way my grandmother had done. With practice you can become fairly quick at it. Then I tried a bead spinner and my world changed! I could now string beads in less than half the time. I actually own several spinners in different sizes and different variations of wood. My favorite spinner has a wire-twisting device at the top of the spindle. I like to use multiple spinners when I am shading, keeping a separate color in each spinner. This may seem excessive to a beginner; but once you try a bead spinner, there's no going back! If you make only one expensive purchase for all your supplies, this is where I would put my money. It makes all the difference in the enjoyment you will get out of creating these projects. Remember, there are a lot of beads in each flower. It is much more fun to make the flowers than to string the beads onto the wire.

Straw-colored, brown, and white floral tapes; non-hardening modeling clay; assorted green floral tapes.

## OTHER SUPPLIES

Floral tape—to assemble the projects. Floral tape is available in many colors and can be selected by how well the color matches the beads, or by how realistic it will make your stems appear.

Nonhardening modeling clay—to support potted flowers. Some projects will require that you "pot" the flowers in a container or vessel. Because beaded flowers are very heavy, they require a strong support within the container. Dry oasis, found in the floral department of a craft store, will not support the weight of the beaded flowers. I recommend using a nonhardening modeling clay, which can also be found in most craft stores. Nonhardening modeling clay can be purchased in bulk or when it is on sale. It is also available in many different colors.

## GENERAL TIPS

Always work with the beads from the spool. This will prevent you from running out of wire in the middle of a petal or leaf.

Always make a knot in the end of the spool wire after beading to prevent the beads from falling off. This sounds so simple and so basic, but I cannot tell you how many times even the most experienced beaders will get so caught up in what they are working on that they let go of that wire for just one split second. Next thing you know, you are down on your knees hunting down every last one of those three-cut beads because they were your last hank of that special garnet red.

Work under good lighting conditions. There are several specialty light bulbs available in craft stores that make beading much easier on the eyes and emphasize the beautiful colors.

When cutting beads off the hank to put into the bead spinner, cut beads inside a reclosable plastic bag, then transfer them to the bowl of the spinner. You will lose a lot fewer beads this way.

To get the beads out of the spinner, a sandwich-size bag will usually fit over the spindle and the bowl. Simply turn the spinner upside down, inside the bag.

When stringing beads, prevent the wire from unraveling off the spool by placing it inside a smaller reclosable bag and zipping the top closed with the wire sticking out. You can then pull out as much wire as needed without the spool becoming a slinky. Save the bags from your floral tape or from individual hanks of beads.

▪ NEVER cut the wire off the spool after you have strung your beads onto the wire unless the directions specifically tell you how many inches of bare wire to leave before you cut.

▪ When you see a color bead that you really like, especially odd shades, buy as much of it as you can afford at the time, or buy as much as is available at the time. You never know when, or if, you will see that same color bead again.

▪ As your collection of seed beads grows, keep a small sample of your colors on short pieces of wire hooked together so that you can take them with you when you shop. This will help you avoid purchasing duplicate quantities of some colors. Or, it may help you to match a certain color if you are in low supply.

▪ When reaching the assembly stage of making a flower, your hands will become sticky from the glue of the floral tape. Try to avoid the temptation to shape your petals until you have put the entire flower together and have had time to wash your hands. The glue from the tape will make the beads dull and the petals sticky. Baby wipes work wonders to remove glue from your hands.

▪ Keep the flowers looking sparkly and dust-free by dipping a cotton swab into a small container of window cleaner and gently wiping the petals and leaves. It will be easy to get into all the crevices of the petals with the tip of the swab. The beads will sparkle like new.

## Getting Started

The first step in making the flowers and projects on the following pages is to transfer the beads to the wire. There are two ways to do this. The first is a little more time consuming, but it works. If the beads are on strings, wrap one end of the string around the pointer finger of your nondominant hand. Keeping the beads in a tight straight line, insert the wire into the beads with your dominant hand. Pull the beads off the wire. Continue until you have the required number of inches of beads on the wire in order to start the flower.

Stringing the beads by hand

The second way to transfer beads to the wire is to pour loose beads into the bowl of a bead spinner and spin the beads onto the wire. If you are starting with your beads on the hank, cut the beads off the strings inside a plastic bag, then pour the beads into the bowl of the spinner. If the beads are already loose, transfer them to the bowl.

Make a curve at the end of the wire. You can use the spindle of the spinner to get a smooth curve. Hold the curve of the wire down into the beads. As you twist the spindle with your other hand, hold the curve of the wire facing down and just skim the top surface of the beads. If you lift the wire out of the bowl, the beads on the wire will fall back into the bowl. If you press too far down and hit the bottom of the bowl with the wire, the beads will go flying out of the bowl. It takes a little practice to get the hang of it, but it does not take long before you can send 5"–6" of beads flying up the wire at one time. To keep the beads from falling back into the bowl, before lifting the wire out, let go of the spindle and pinch the end of the wire to secure the beads. Tilt the wire back and send the beads toward the spool.

Stringing the beads, using a bead spinner

# Techniques

French Beaded
Wildflowers

French Beaded
Roses

French Beaded
Daisies

French Beaded
Tulip

French Beaded
Anemones

French Beaded
Hydrangeas

# French Beaded Wildflowers

**What You Need to Know:**
No experience necessary

**What You Will Learn:**
Round Basic
Pointed Basic
Continuous Loops
Simple Flower Assembly

## Materials (for Petals)

- Size 11° seed beads* in any color (3 strands)
- 24- or 26-gauge colored copper wire** in coordinating color

## Materials (for Center)

- Size 11° seed beads* in coordinating color (1 strand)
- 24- or 26-gauge colored copper in coordinating color**

## Materials (for Calyx & Leaves)

- Size 11° seed beads: green (2 strands)
- 24- or 26-gauge colored copper wire in coordinating color

## Other Supplies

- 18-gauge stem wire (10" piece)
- 30-gauge paddle wire: green, or 28-gauge assembly wire: silver
- Floral tape: green

## Tools

- General Tools on page 12

*Size 9° three-cut beads may be substituted for size 11° seed beads.
**Beginners should use 24-gauge wire. This is a stiffer wire and will hold its shape more easily.*

## Making the Petals

**Pattern: Make 5**     Basic 4, 9 Rows, RTRB
Trim petal stems so one long wire extends

1. String 9" of the beads on the 24- or 26-gauge, colored copper wire.

   In order to create a majority of the flowers, using the French technique, it is necessary to first master the technique for "Creating the Framework" upon which the leaves or petals will be made. This framework is called the "Basic" and includes the top basic wire, the basic beads, and the stem. The basic beads are the number of beads indicated in a pattern as "basic" followed by a number. For example: Basic 4. It is the number of beads used to start the pattern, and will vary from pattern to pattern.

   The basic wire is the portion of wire upon which the beads float. The stem is the portion of wire that is twisted below the basic beads and includes the loop. The spool wire is the wire that is attached to the spool and contains the beads that you are using to create the petals or leaves. (Photo 1)

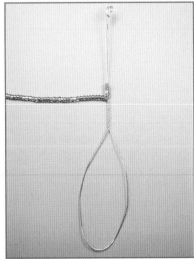
Photo 1

Photo 2

Photo 3

Photo 4

**TIP**

*When wrapping the spool wire around the basic wire, press the wire down close to the beads with your fingernail. This will keep the rows nice and tight and will avoid the spaces between the rows of the petal.*

2. Create the basic framework as follows:

   **a.** Slide the required number of basic beads up toward the knot. Hold your thumb and forefinger at 3" from the end of the knot to prevent the beads from slipping back. The wildflower pattern requires a basic of four beads.

   **b.** Keeping the spool to your right and the knot to your left, make a loop by bringing bare wire around to meet your thumb and forefinger. Twist the loop wire tightly together several times. The number of twists should equal the number of rows required in the leaf or petal.

   **c.** Hold the wire so the knot is the top and the loop is the bottom. The beads will slip down and rest against the twist in the lower loop. Be certain the basic wire (the wire holding the beads) and the twisted wire (the stem) are always in a straight line.

3. Make a Round Petal. *Note: A pattern will indicate that a petal or leaf is to be round by using the words "round top," or "round bottom," or the abbreviations "RT" or "RB." The top refers to the basic wire end and the bottom refers to the stem wire end.* To make a petal that is round top round bottom, or RTRB, complete the following steps:

   **a.** Create the basic, using the required number of basic beads called for in the pattern. In the case of the wildflower, this is four beads.

   **b.** Bring the spool wire with some beads on it up along the left side of the basic, using enough beads to fit closely together alongside the basic, starting at the bottom of the first bead and continuing along to the top of the basic beads. (Photo 2)

   **c.** Holding both rows of beads firmly near the top, cross bare wire in front of the top basic wire. Bring the wire around to the back, then cross in front again to make a complete circle around the top basic wire. Keep this wire at a 90-degree angle to the basic wire as you wrap. This will make the petal round.

   **d.** Continue the petal by sliding more beads up to the basic. Turn the petal upside down so the stem wire is now on top and the basic wire is pointing down. (Photo 3)

   **e.** Be certain to keep the face of the petal toward you as you turn it upside down. Think of turning it the way that a windmill turns, keeping the front of the petal facing you, as you turn it to the side. Use enough beads to fit snugly against the other side of the basic beads. Cross the spool wire in front of the basic wire and wrap around to the back and return to the front, always keeping the wrapping wire at a 90-degree angle to the stem wire. Once you have completed the wrap, slide more beads up to make the next row. (Photo 4)

f. Continue working around the petal in this manner until the required number of rows has been completed. The number of rows in a pattern is usually an odd number to allow you to finish at the stem wire end. The rows are counted across the petal and include the basic row. The wildflower petal has nine rows across. (Photo 5)

g. After completing the last row, twist the spool wire around the stem wire approximately three times, making the wire end up at the top of the loop. Cut the wire from the spool, being certain to hold onto the spool wire. Immediately make a knot in the spool wire before proceeding further so that no beads are lost. Leave 1" of wire from the point where the spool wire meets the loop. (Photo 6)

h. To "Trim the petal wire so that one long wire extends," cut one side of the loop wire approximately 2" from the petal, creating three wires, which when twisted together will reduce to one long wire. Straighten the loop wire and twist all three wires into one stem. (Photos 7 & 8)

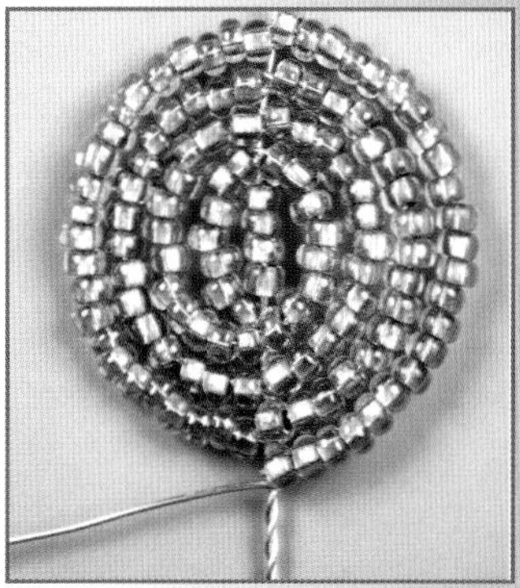

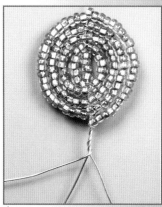

Photo 5

Photo 6

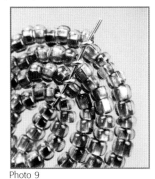

Photo 7

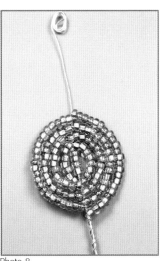

Photo 8

i. Cut the basic wire at the top of the petal ⅛" from the petal. Using round-nosed pliers, bend wire flat toward the back of the petal. *Note: The back of the petal will be the side that shows the twisted wire running down the center of the petal.* (Photos 9 & 10)

Photo 9

Photo 10

**NOTE**

*Be certain the basic wire (the wire holding the beads) and the twisted wire (the stem) are always in a straight line.*

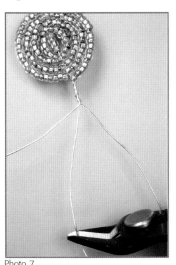

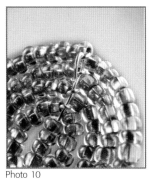

Photo 11

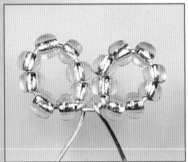

Photo 12

Photo 13

Photo 14

4. Make a total of five petals.

## Making the Center

> **NOTE**
>
> There are two parts to the center: the inner center and the outer center.

**Pattern for Inner Center: Make 1    2 continuous 8-bead loops**

> **NOTE**
>
> Continuous loops are a series of loops made one after another on the same wire.

1. String 16 beads on the wire. Make a single loop with eight beads. To make the single loop, slide the required number of beads to within 3" of the knot. Make a circle with the beads, crossing the spool wire over the top as you make the loop. Twist the loop, two half-turns, beneath the circle of beads. (Photo 11)

2. Slide eight more beads for the second loop close to the base of the first loop. Insert your thumbnail in between the first loop and the beads for the second loop. *Note: This will allow just enough space to twist the second loop without crossing over the first loop.* Make a second circle with the beads, crossing the wire over the top as you make the loop. Twist the second loop, two half twists, beneath the circle of beads. (Photo 12)

> **TIP**
>
> Be certain to twist all the loops in the same direction as you make each one. This will prevent the loops from opening up when you assemble the flower

3. Cut the spool wire 3" from the last loop. Twist the two end wires together to form a stem. (Photo 13)

4. Press the two loops together so that they stand straight up, face to face. Set aside until the outer center is made. (Photo 14)

**Pattern for Outer Center: Make 1**          **5 continuous 1" loops**

1. String 5" of beads on the wire. Measure 1" of beads. Make the first loop 3" from the knot. Twist the loop two half turns to secure. (Photo 15)

2. Measure another 1" of beads. Insert your thumbnail in between the first loop and the beads for the second loop. This will allow just enough space to twist the second loop without crossing over the first loop. Make a second circle with the beads. Twist the loop two half-turns to secure.

3. Continue making 1" continuous loops until you have made five loops. (Photo 16)

4. Insert the two-loop center into the middle of the five-loop center and twist the wires tightly underneath the petals. Arrange the five loops so they are evenly spaced around the center. (Photo 17)

Photo 15

Photo 16

# Making the Calyx

**Pattern: Make 1**          **5 continuous 1¼" loops, leaving ¼" between each loop**

1. String 6¼" of beads on the wire. Measure 1¼" of beads for the first loop. Make the first loop 3" from the knot.

2. Measure another 1¼" of beads. Start the second loop ¼" from the base of the first loop. Twist the second loop two half turns to secure. *Note: There will now be a little less than ¼" of wire between the two loops. The bare wire that is left between each loop will allow the calyx to wrap completely around the stem underneath the petals of the flower. Once the stem has been taped with floral tape, the wire in between the loops will not be visible.*

3. Continue making each loop, leaving ¼" of bare wire in between each loop, until five loops have been made. Cut the spool wire 3" from the last loop. Do not twist the stem wires together. Set aside until assembly. (Photo 18)

Photo 17

Photo 18

**TIP**

*The centers of the wildflower may be used as flowers all by themselves. Group several together for a cute miniature arrangement or use to adorn hair accessories.*

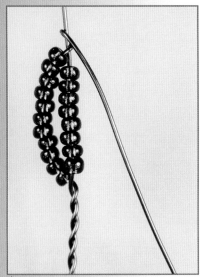
Photo 19

Photo 20

Photo 21

## Making the Leaves

**Pattern: Make 3**     **Basic 8, 7 Rows, PTRB**
**Cut stem wires so that three wires extend**

1. Make a pointed leaf. *Note: A pattern will indicate that a petal or leaf is to be pointed by using the words "pointed top" or "pointed bottom," or the abbreviations "PT" or "PB." To make a leaf that is pointed top, round bottom or PTRB, complete the following steps:*

2. Making a point on the leaf is similar to making a round petal except when wrapping the wire around the basic. To make a point, the wire will wrap across the basic or stem wire at a 45-degree angle. When the wire comes back around from the back to the front, the angle will allow for one more bead to sit higher than the previous row, thus creating a point. (Photo 19)

### TIP

*Do not press the wire down close to the top of the beads as you do when you make a round petal. To make a pointed leaf, it is important to leave some space above the last bead at the top of the leaf. This is where most students fail when making points. Do not be afraid to leave space as you wrap the spool wire around the basic wire.*

3. When starting a new row, push the beads to the basic, making certain one bead sits at the very top, in the space that was left when you wrapped the wire at the 45-degree angle, above the row you just finished. (Photo 20)

4. Turn the leaf so the loop end is at the top (remember the windmill). Make the bottom of the leaf round by wrapping the wire around the stem end at a 90-degree angle. (Photo 21)

5. Continue wrapping around the basic, pointed at the top and round at the bottom until all seven rows have been made. When you have finished the correct number of rows you will be on the bottom of the leaf. (Photo 22)

Photo 22

**Review:** When a pattern calls for a PTRB, it is important to distinguish between the top of the leaf and the bottom. Remember that the basic wire is always the top and the stem wire (with the loop) is always the bottom. Wrap the wire around the basic wire at a 45-degree angle and wrap around the stem wire at a 90-degree angle. This is the shape common to many leaves. The secret to making good points is to remember to leave a little space above the row you just finished when wrapping the wire at the 45-degree angle. This will allow the next row to sit one bead higher than the previous row.

6. Wrap the spool wire around the stem wire approximately three times until the wire sits at the top of the loop.

7. When a pattern calls for three wires to extend, cut the spool wire so it will be as long as the loop, then cut the loop in the middle to leave two equal length wires. (Photo 23)

8. Twist all three wires together to form a stem. The thickness of the three equal lengths of wire will give strength to the stem, allowing these wires to be used as stem wires alone, without the need to attach them to additional floral stem wire. Cut the top basic wire 1/8" from top of the leaf and press it to the back of the leaf. Remember the back is the side with the twisted wire running down the center of the leaf.

Photo 23

## Assembling the Wildflower

1. Tape the 18-gauge stem wire. Pull the tape as you wrap to activate the glue in the tape. (Photo 24)

2. Attach the center to the tip of the stem wire with 30-gauge wire or 28-gauge wire so that the stem wire is just beneath the beaded loops. Keep the paddle wire just beneath the loops of the center. (Photo 25)

3. Bend each petal at a 90-degree angle so that the good side faces up. (Photo 26)

4. Attach each petal, face up, one at a time, by wrapping assembly wire around each of the petal stems and the stem wire. Wrap each petal approximately three times before adding the next petal. (Photo 27)

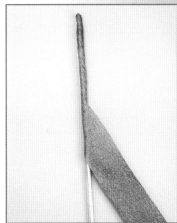
Photo 24

Photo 25

Photo 26

Photo 27

Photo 28

Photo 29

Photo 30

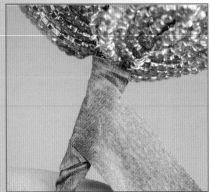
Photo 31

5. Keep the assembly wire just below the petal until all five petals have been added. Place each of the five petals so that there is some overlap as they surround the center. (Photo 28)

6. When all five petals have been attached, wrap the assembly wire tightly around the stem approximately ¼" below the petals. Cut the assembly wire. (Photo 29)

7. Trim the petal wires so that there will be less bulk along the main flower stem. Stagger the lengths of the wire so that you don't end up with a ridge where all the wires end. Cut the first wire about ½" from the petals and work around the stem, trimming off the excess lengths of wire. (Photo 30)

8. Tape the stem beneath the petals to cover the petal wires. (Photo 31)

9. Circle the five loops of the calyx around the stem and twist the two tail wires together to secure. (Photo 32)

Photo 32

10. Bend the stem of the calyx flat against the stem of the flower. Tape the stem, covering the calyx wires. Continue to tape the entire stem. (Photo 33)

11. Tape each individual leaf, using half the width of the floral tape. (Photo 34)

Photo 33

Photo 34

12. Tape the first leaf to the main flower stem approximately 2" below the flower head. Leave 1" of the leaf stem protruding from the main flower stem. (Photo 35)

13. Add the second leaf ½" below the first, then the third leaf another ½" below the second leaf. Circle the second and third leaves around the stem so that all the leaves are not on one side of the flower. Continue taping down the remainder of the stem. (Photo 36)

14. Shape the flower by cupping the petals up. Bend the calyx loops down, away from the flower head. Gently arch the leaves away from the flower head. Tilt the flower head by bending the stem slightly, approximately 1" below the petals. (Photo 37)

If you have completed the French Beaded Wildflower, you may want to try these projects:

Napkin Ring on page 62
Mistletoe Ball on page 112
Christmas Tree on page 118

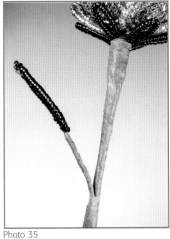

Photo 35

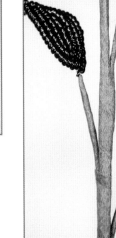

Photo 36

Photo 37

# French Beaded Roses

**What You Need to Know:**
Round Basic on page 18
Pointed Basic on page 22

**What You Will Learn:**
Lacing
Reverse Wrap

## Materials (for Petals)

■ Size 11° seed beads; or size 9° three-cut beads: red (2 hanks)
■ 24- or 26-gauge colored copper wire in coordinating color (1 spool)
■ 30-gauge colored copper wire in coordinating color (1 spool)

## Materials (for Sepals & Leaves)

■ Size 11° seed beads, green (2 hanks)
■ 24-gauge colored copper wire in coordinating color (1 spool)
■ 30-gauge colored copper wire in coordinating color (1 spool)

## Other Supplies

■ 16-gauge stem wire (3 pieces)
■ 18-gauge stem wire
■ 30-gauge paddle wire: green; or 28-gauge assembly: silver (1 spool)
■ Floral tape: green

## Tools

■ General Tools on page 12

## Making the Petals

| Patterns: Make 2 | Basic 6, 11 Rows, RTRB |
|---|---|
| Make 2 | Basic 6, 15 Rows, RTRB |
| Make 2 | Basic 6, 17 Rows, RTRB<br>Trim so one long wire extends<br>Lace* all petals |

*Lacing is done on petals which are either very large in width, very long in length, or if the petals need to be shaped by excessive folding and rolling, as in the case of roses. Lacing is a way of sewing the rows of beads together with a very thin wire, so that they will not separate. *Note: As a general rule, lace all petals that have 13 rows or more. In the case of French Beaded Roses, all the petals are laced because they need to be either folded or rolled along the edges.*

1. Make all petals round on the top and round on the bottom. (Photo 1)

2. To lace the petals, start with a piece of 30-gauge wire that is approximately five times the width of the petal you are about to lace. At a minimum, work with 6" of wire for easy manipulation. Begin with the petal facing right side up and insert one end of the wire on one side of the basic row and the other end of the wire on the other side of the basic row. Pull the ends toward the back of the petal. (Photo 2)

Photo 1

Photo 2

Photo 3

Photo 4

3. On the wrong side of the petal, cross the two wires around the basic beads, securing them in between the two center beads on the basic row. (Photo 3)

4. Begin by turning the petal sideways and working from the center to the outer edge of the petal. When finished with one side, turn the petal and work from the center to the other outer edge of the petal. Be certain you are working on the wrong side of the petal. This will make the lacing almost invisible from the right side of the petal.

5. Hold the petal so the basic row is horizontal. Starting from the center and working to the top outer edge, take the wire bending up and insert it over the top of the next row. The wire is now on the right side of the petal. (Photo 4)

6. Bring the wire back to the wrong side by coming underneath the row you just went over. Pull the wire taut so that it is secure between two beads on that row. You have now "sewn" your first row. (Photo 5)

7. Continue by going over the top of the next row and coming back to the wrong side underneath that next row. Lace each row including the outer edge of the petal. *Note: Try to make the "stitches" move in a straight line by fitting the wire in between beads that are directly above the ones you chose on the row below. This is not always easy, especially with cut beads, as the size of beads can often vary significantly.*

8. When reaching the last row, wrap the wire around the row twice in the same place (between the same two beads), securing the lacing wire. Trim the lacing wire very close to the last row of beads. *Note: The wire will not unravel if it was wrapped twice between two beads.* (Photo 6)

Photo 5

Photo 6

9. Turn the petal and begin lacing from the middle to the other edge of the petal. *Note: Lacing from the center to the outer edge is done to avoid cinching the petal across the center. It is easier to distort the shape of the petal if you begin on one side and work your way across the entire width of the petal, than if you start in the center and work out to the edges.*

The view of the petal from the wrong side will show the lacing wire, while the view from the right side of the petal will show very little lacing wire.

## Making the Last Five Petals

**Pattern: Make 5**     **Basic 6, 21 Rows, RTRB**
**Reverse wrap\* at bottom**
**Trim so one long wire extends**
**Lace all petals**

\*Reverse wrap at the bottom will create a petal that does not show any ridges of wire on the outside when the flower is assembled. It is a nice way of finishing off the flower. To reverse wrap at the bottom, it is important to remember that the loop end of the basic frame is the bottom of the petal.

1. To reverse wrap bottom, bring the wire around to the back before wrapping around the basic wire. Keep the wrap at a 90-degree angle to keep the petal round even though you started the wrap from behind the basic wire. *Note: Nothing else changes when making the petal. At the top, the wire crosses in front of the basic wire, at the bottom it crosses behind the basic wire.*

**NOTE**

*Lacing enables you to create petals and leaves that are solid and full, and allows you to create shapes that achieve more realistic looking flowers.*

**TIP**

*There are many shades of 30-gauge colored copper wire on the market. Select a color that closely matches the color beads of your petals. This will help to make the lacing wire disappear into the petal. If the color you are looking for is not available in 30 gauge, try using 32-gauge wire. This is a thinner wire and can break if pulled too hard. Adjust the tension when using 32 gauge. 34-gauge wire is also available, but this is so thin that it almost always breaks. If possible, avoid using 34 gauge wire for lacing.*

Photo 7

Photo 8

2. When the reverse wrap is finished, notice the bottom of the petal front will show wire ridges. (Photo 7)

3. To lace a petal that has a reverse wrap at the bottom, remember to work on the wrong side of the petal, which is the side that has the ridges at the top. Lace the remaining petals. (Photo 8)

## Making the Sepals

**Pattern: Make 5**   **Basic 9, 3 Rows, RTRB with a twist**
**Trim so one long wire extends**

1. Make the basic frame with a top basic wire that is 2" long. Start making each sepal the way that you would normally make a petal that is Basic 9, 3 Rows, RTRB.

2. After the third row, cut the knot off the top of the basic wire and add 11 beads to the basic wire. (Photo 9)

3. Make the fourth and fifth rows by following around the shape of the petal plus the added basic beads. Make these rows PTRB. Trim so one long wire extends. Trim the top basic wire ⅛" and bend to the back of the sepal. (Photo 10)

4. At the point where the 11 beads were added to the basic wire, twist the leaf a couple times. Half of the sepal will be flat like an ordinary leaf and the top half will be twisted to the point. Set aside until assembly. (Photo 11)

Photo 9

Photo 10

Photo 11

# Making the Leaves

**Patterns: Make 1**  **Basic 6, 21 Rows, PTRB**

**Make 3**  **Basic 6, 17 Rows, PTRB**

**Make 2**  **Basic 6, 15 Rows, PTRB**

**Make 2**  **Basic 12, 11 Rows, PTRB**
**Trim so one long wire extends**
**Lace all leaves (Photo 12)**

Photo 12

# Assembling the Rose

1. Wrap three pieces of 16-gauge wire individually with floral tape. Tape the three wires together to make one stem wire. (Photo 13)

2. Fold the two 11-row petals in half down the center with the right side facing out. Join the two petals together by interlocking the petals and twisting the stem wires together. (Photo 14)

3. Attach these two petals to the top of the stem with 30-gauge wire or 28-gauge wire wire. Keep the wire at the top of the stem just beneath the petals. *Note: This will become the center of the rose.* (Photo 15)

Photo 13

Photo 14

Photo 15

Photo 16

4. Place the two 15-row petals opposite each other, surrounding the center. The front of the petals face in toward the center. (Photo 16)

5. Next, place the two 17-row petals opposite each other in the spaces left by the previous two petals. (Photo 17)

Photo 17

French Beaded Roses 31

Photo 18

Photo 19

Photo 20

Photo 21

6. For the petals that were reverse wrapped, the right side, which faces in, is the side where the top of the petal shows no wire. Continue adding the last five petals around the rose, overlapping each petal slightly. (Photo 18)

7. When the last petal has been attached, wrap the assembly wire down the stem approximately ¼" and cut from the spool. Taper some of the wires to reduce the bulk around the stem. Stagger the length of the wires so that a ridge will not appear when the stem is taped. (Photo 19)

8. Tape the stem. Be certain to tape right up to the bottom of the petals. Tape down to the center of the stem.

9. Add the sepals one at a time with floral tape. Place the right side against the rose petals. When all five sepals have been added, continue taping down the remaining length of the stem to cover all the wires. (Photo 20)

10. Cut two 9" pieces of 18-gauge wire. Tape each wire. Make two branches of leaves with the first branch containing five leaves. Start with the leaf containing 21 rows and attach it to the top of the first stem wire. (Photo 21)

11. Bend the wires of two 17-row leave at right angles to the leaves. Bend one to the right and one to the left. (Photo 22)

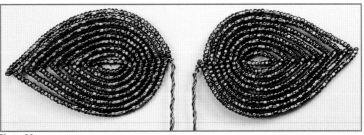

Photo 22

12. Add the two 17-row leaves approximately 1" below the first leaf, directly opposite each other. Tape so that no stem wire from the leaves shows. (Photo 23)

Photo 23

13. Attach the two leaves with 12 beads in the basic approximately 1" below the 17-row leaves, directly opposite each other. Bend the wires at right angles to the leaves and attach in the same manner that you attached the 17-row leaves. Continue taping down the remainder of the stem.

14. Make the second branch of leaves with the remaining leaves. Attach the 17-row leaf to the top of the second stem wire. Bend the wires of the two 15-row leaves at right angles to the leaves, one to the left and one to the right. Attach these two leaves approximately 1" below the 17-row leaf. Continue taping down the remainder of the stem. (Photo 24)

15. Attach the leaf branches to the main flower stem. Attach the branch with three leaves 6" below the petals with floral tape. Leave 2"–3" of leaf wire showing. (Photo 25)

16. Attach the second branch below the first, on the opposite side of the main stem. Continue taping down the entire length of the stem. (Photo 26)

17. Shape all petals and leaves with gentle curves and bends to achieve a natural look. Curve the top of the stem just beneath the flower head. Bend the sepals down toward the leaves and make them curly and wild. (Photo 27)

Photo 24

Photo 25

Photo 27

Photo 26

If you have completed the French Beaded Roses, you may want to try these projects:
    Rose Topiary on page 67
    Fall Berry Wreath on page 103

# French Beaded Daisies

**What You Need to Know:**
Round Basic on page 18
Pointed Basic on page 22
Continuous Loops on page 20
Lacing on page 26

**What You Will Learn:**
Continuous 4-row Crossover
Beehive Basic
Loopback Technique

## Materials (for Petals)

■ Size 9° three-cut beads*: white
(1 hank for three flowers)
■ 24- or 26-gauge assembly
wire**: white (1 spool)

## Materials (for Center)

■ Size 11° seed beads*: yellow
(1 hank)
■ 24- or 26-gauge colored copper:
gold, lemon, or yellow

## Materials (for Calyx & Leaves)

■ Size 11° seed beads*: light or
medium green (1 hank)
■ 24- or 26-gauge colored copper
wire: green
■ 30- or 32-gauge colored copper
wire for lacing: green

## Other Supplies

■ 16-gauge stem wire
■ Floral tape: light green

## Tools

■ General Tools on page 12

*Size 9° three-cut beads and size 11°
seed beads are interchangeable in
this pattern.
**Silver colored copper wire may be
substituted for white craft wire. At
this time, pure white wire is not
available in colored copper wire.

## Making the Petals

**Pattern: Make 1**      **12 continuous 2" 4-row crossover loops**

1. String 48" of white beads on the wire. Measure 2" of beads and make a loop
3" from the knot in the wire. Make the loop long and narrow. (Photo 1)

2. Slide enough beads to go up the center of the loop. When you get to the
top of the loop, push the excess beads away. (Photo 2)

3. Bend the bare wire over the top of the loop and slide enough beads to go
down the other side of the loop. Make certain that there are no beads at
the top of the loop. *Note: Bare wire must cross over the top of the loop and lock in
between two beads of the first loop. This will keep the crossover loops from coming
apart during assembly.* (Photo 3)

Photo 1

Photo 2

Photo 3

Photo 4

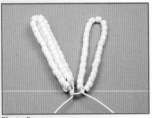
Photo 5

Photo 6

Photo 7

4. When you get to the bottom of the loop, push away the excess beads. Wrap the spool wire around the bottom of the loop two times. Finish with the spool wire on the right side of the 4-row crossover loop. (Photo 4)

5. Make a second crossover loop. Measure 2" of beads and start the next loop ⅛" from the first loop. Continue the 4-row crossover the same way that you made the first one. (Photo 5)

6. Continue making the 4-row crossovers until you have completed 12 loops. *Note: It is helpful to work in one direction, keeping the completed loops to your left and adding each consecutive loop to the right of the last completed loop. This will help keep all the wires twisting in the same direction and prevent any loops from opening up during assembly.* (Photo 6)

7. After 12 continuous crossover loops have been made, cut the spool wire, leaving a 3" tail. Close the circle of crossover loops by twisting the two tail wires together to form one stem. (Photo 7)

## Making the Center

**Pattern: Make 1**     **Basic 3, 10 Rows, RTRB**
                        **Form a beehive basic**

1. String 8" of yellow beads on the wire. Make the top basic wire 3" long and create a loop that is also 3" long when the loop is closed. Start the first two rows of the center, making the top and bottom both round. (Photo 8)

2. After completing the first two rows, bend the top basic wire and the stem wire almost perpendicular to the beads. The wires should slant a little, but point down. (Photo 9)

3. Continue wrapping the next row by bringing the beads slightly underneath the first row. Remember to keep the RTRB shape as you wrap each row by keeping the spool wire at a 90-degree angle to the basic wire, even though the wire is bent down. (Photo 10)

Photo 8

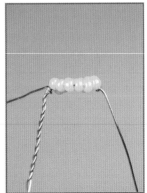
Photo 9

Photo 10

4. Once Rows 3 and 4 are completed, place your finger inside the beehive as you wrap around the basic wires. This will help to develop the beehive shape. (Photo 11)

5. Continue until 10 rows have been completed. The last row will finish at the top basic wire end, rather than at the loop end as with other petals. Twist the spool wire and the basic wire together approximately 1". Cut the spool wire the same length as the basic wire. Cut the loop end open at the bottom of the loop and twist these two wires together approximately 1". (Photo 12)

6. Bend the two wires underneath the beehive and twist them together in the center of the beehive to form one stem wire. (Photo 13)

Photo 11

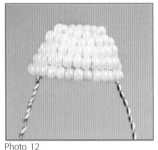
Photo 12

Photo 13

## Making the Calyx

**Pattern: Make 1          12 continuous 1" loops**

1. String 12" of green beads on the wire. Leave a 3" tail at both ends. Make 12 continuous 1" loops.

2. Twist the two end wires together approximately 1" to close the circle of loops.

3. Cup the loops. (Photo 14)

Photo 14

## Making the Leaves

**Pattern: Make 3          Basic 1¼", 5 Rows, RBPT,**
**followed by four loops, made on alternating**
**sides with the loopback technique**
**Use 3¼" of green beads for Loop 1 and 2**
**Use 2¾" of green beads for Loop 3 and 4**
**Trim so three long wires extend**

1. Start the leaf as you would make an ordinary leaf that has a basic of 1¼". Make the first five rows RBPT. (Photo 15)

Photo 15

Photo 16

Photo 17

Photo 18

Photo 19

2. Make the first loop on the left side with 3¼" of beads. Start the loop by bringing the beads up the leaf. Swing the loop out to the left and back down to the bottom of the leaf. Wrap wire around the bottom stem wire after each loop. (Photo 16)

3. Make the second loop on the right side of the leaf. Measure 3¼" of beads. Start the loop by bringing the beads up the leaf. Swing the loop out to the right and back down to the bottom of the leaf. (Photo 17)

4. Make the third loop on the left side of the leaf. Measure 2¾" of beads and make the loop beneath the first loop. Swing the loop to the outside of the leaf. Make the fourth loop on the right side of the leaf with 2¾" of beads. Trim so that three long wires extend. (Photo 18)

Photo 20

5. Pull the loops up alongside the main part of the leaf. *Note: This will elongate the loops.* (Photo 19)

6. Lace each leaf in two places. First lace across the bottom of the leaf, making certain to catch all the loops in the lacing; then lace across the top half of the leaf, making certain not to catch the bottom two loops.

7. Tape each leaf, using half the width of the floral tape. (Photo 20)

## Assembling the Daisy

1. Tape the stem wire.

2. Attach the center of the flower to the stem wire with the floral tape. After attaching, cut the floral tape from the spool. Wrap the wire around the bottom stem wire after each loop. *Note: This will allow the petals and calyx to slip onto the stem easier.* (Photo 21)

3. Attach the petals. Slide the petals up the stem wire until the petals meet the center. *Note: The stem wire will not be in the center of the open hole at the bottom of the flower. This is OK.* Attach the petals with floral tape. Cut the tape from the spool when the petals are attached. (Photo 22)

Photo 21

Photo 22

4. Slide the calyx up the stem and push up to get it as close to the petals as possible. *Note: This will help hold up the petals and keep them closer to the center.* Tape the calyx to the stem wire. Continue taping down the stem until all the wires have been covered. (Photo 23)

5. Attach the leaves one at a time to the main stem of the flower. Place the first leaf several inches below the flower. Leave 1" of the leaf stem wire protruding from the main flower stem. (Photo 24)

6. Attach the remaining two leaves below the first leaf, circling the stem of the flower. (Photo 25)

7. Shape the petals of the flower by pressing the petals down toward the leaves in approximately the center of each petal. Bend the stem of the flower so that the head tilts a little. Shape each of the three leaves by bending them in approximately the center of each leaf. (Photo 26)

Photo 23

Photo 24

Photo 25

Photo 26

If you have completed the French Beaded Daisies, you may want to try these projects:

Black Tie Candleholders on page 71
Forsythia Urn on page 75
Wheat Votives on page 108

TECHNIQUES

# French Beaded Tulip

**What You Need to Know:**
Round Basic on page 18
Pointed Basic on page 22
Lacing on page 26

**What You Will Learn:**
Scalloped Edges
Lace-as-You-Go
Beaded Stems

## Materials (for Petals)

- Size 11° seed beads; or size 9° three-cut beads: pearl (2 hanks)
- 26-gauge colored copper wire in coordinating color (12 yds)
- 30-gauge colored copper wire in coordinating color (1 spool)

## Materials (for Centers)

- Size 11° seed beads; or size 9° three-cut beads: white, beige, pale yellow, or very pale green (1 strand)
- Size 11° seed beads; or size 9° three-cut beads: brown (1 strand)
- 26-gauge colored copper wire in coordinating color (3 yds)

## Materials (for Leaves & Stem)

- Size 11° seed beads: green* (2 hanks)
- 24-gauge colored copper wire in coordinating color (10 yds)
- 26-gauge colored copper wire in coordinating color (3 yds)
- 30-gauge colored copper wire in coordinating color (1 spool)

## Other Supplies

- 12" length of 18-gauge stem wire (3); or 16-gauge stem wire for longer flowers (3)
- 30-gauge paddle wire: green; or 28-gauge assembly wire: silver
- Floral tapes: light floral green; white floral tape**
- Masking tape

## Tools

- General Tools on page 12

*Cut beads do not work well for wrapping stems; therefore, I recommend that size 11° seed beads be used so that the leaves and stem are all in the same color.*
**White floral tape is only needed if your petal color is very light.*

## Making the Petals

**Pattern: Make 6**    **Basic 12, 15 Rows, RBPT**
**Make two scallops on each side, ½" apart**
**Lace across all rows**

Photo 1

Photo 2

1. String 30" of beads on the wire. Make a petal that is RBPT and contains 15 rows. (Photo 1)

2. After row 15, cut off 24" of bare wire from the spool. Add enough beads to continue row 16, stopping approximately ½" from the point of the petal. From the back side of the petal, push the wire through in between the last two outer rows of the petal. Make certain that the new row stays flat alongside the last row of the petal. Pull the wire through to the front and secure it in between two beads in the same manner as you would if you were lacing a petal. Refer to Lacing on page 26. (Photo 2)

Photo 3

Photo 4

Photo 5

3. With the wire in the front of the petal, add enough beads to go back down alongside the row that you just made. Wrap the wire once around the bottom of the petal. (Photo 3)

4. Make a scallop on the other side of the petal by adding enough beads to stop approximately ½" from the point of the petal. From the back side of the petal, push the wire through in between the last two outer rows on this side of the petal. Pull the wire through to the front and secure it between two beads. With the wire in the front of the petal, add enough beads to go back down alongside the row that you just made. Wrap the wire once around the bottom of the petal. (Photo 4)

5. Make a second scallop on the left side of the petal. Continue by adding enough beads to stop approximately ½" from the top of the first scalloped edge. Finish the row in the same manner as the first scallop. (Photo 5)

6. Make the last scallop on the other side of the petal, stopping approximately ½" from the top of the first scalloped edge on this side. Finish the row at the bottom of the petal. Wrap the wire three times at the base of the petal before trimming the wires. Trim so one long wire extends. (Photo 6)

7. Lace each petal across all rows. (Photo 7)

Photo 6

Photo 7

## Making the Stamens

**Pattern: Make 6**     **1½" loop on a 1" stem**

1. String 1½" of brown beads on the wire. Leaving a 2" tail, make a loop of the brown beads. Twist the loop two half turns to secure. Flatten this loop horizontally, keeping the twisted wire in the center of the horizontal loop. Leave a 3" tail after the loop. (Photo 8)

Photo 8

2. Take the 2" tail wire and wrap it through the loop twice. Wrap the wire between the two beads above the twist, which secures the loop. Trim the 2" tail wire as close to the twist as possible. (Photo 9)

3. Add 1" of light-colored beads on the remaining tail wire and slide them up to meet the loop. Tape the wire under the beads at the base of the horizontal loop. *Note: It is best to use half the width of the tape in order to keep the wire as thin as possible.* (Photo 10)

4. Make a total of six stamens.

## Making the Pistil

**Pattern: Make 1       3 continuous stamens with loops**

1. String 8" of light-colored beads on the wire. Leave a 3" tail and push up 15 beads. Follow the 15 beads with an 8-bead loop. (Photo 11)

2. Push up 15 more beads to meet the loop. Form a loop with the first set of the 15 beads, the small loop and the second set of 15 beads. Twist the wire two half-turns to secure. (Photo 12)

3. Make another continuous loop, starting with 15 beads, followed by an 8-bead loop, then another 15 beads. Secure this loop with two half-turns. (Photo 13)

4. Make a third continuous loop as before. Secure this loop with two half-turns. Leave a 3" tail at the end. (Photo 14)

5. Twist the two tail wires together to form one stem wire. Form the three continuous loops into a triangle and fan out the three small 8-bead loops at the pistil top. (Photo 15)

Photo 9

Photo 10

Photo 11

Photo 12

Photo 13

Photo 14

Photo 15

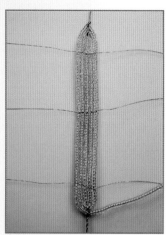

Photo 16

**TIP**

When working with very large leaves, to keep the rows straight and tight, lay the leaf flat on the table as you work to make certain that you do not have too many or too few beads in the row. Once you know that you have the correct number of beads, pick up the leaf to wrap the wire around the basic.

**TIP**

To help keep your basic wire straight as you make any leaf, pull the top basic wire up while pulling down on the loop. Do this every time you wrap a row of beads around the basic wire. This will make a significant difference if the leaf is very large.

## Making the Leaves

**Patterns: Make 1**    Basic 4", 21 Rows, RBPT
Reverse wrap at the bottom of the leaf
Lace in three places, across all rows

       **Make 1**    Basic 5", 27 Rows, RBPT
Reverse wrap at the bottom of the leaf
Lace in three places across all rows

1. To make first leaf, string 114" of green beads on the 24-gauge wire.
2. Lace-as-you-go by beginning to lace after the first two rows are made. Lace each leaf in three places. Cut the lacing wires approximately 12". Continue lacing after every row. Remember that the leaf bottom is reverse wrapped. Therefore, you must lace the bottom on the opposite side from the lacing in the middle and at the top. (Photo 16)
3. To make second leaf, string 192" of green beads on the 24-gauge wire.

## Assembling the Tulip

> **NOTE**
>
> Tulips vary in height; therefore it is possible to make the flower in many lengths. A flower length of more than 12" will require 16-gauge stem wire in order to support the weight. Stem wire in 18-gauge wire will be sufficient if the stems are cut 12" or less.

1. Tape three stem wires individually, then together to form one stem.
2. Tape pistil to the top of the stem wire. *Note: If making a light-colored tulip, use white floral tape so that you will not see any green when you look into the center of the flower.* (Photo 17)
3. Tape the stamens, one at a time, in a circle around the pistil. Trim the stamens wires and tape the stem to cover all wires. (Photo 18)

Photo 17

Photo 18

4. Attach the first three petals with the good side of the petal facing out, one at a time, at the stamen base, using assembly wire. Place each petal so the sides touch each other. Trim and tape the stem wires. (Photo 19)

5. Attach the remaining three petals, using assembly wire. Place each petal in the spaces that were created by the first three petals. Trim the stem wires and tape. (Photo 20)

6. Secure the outer petal edges to the inner petals, using pieces of lacing wire. Tie together in as many places as necessary to give the tulip the desired shape. (Photo 21)

7. Use the light green floral tape to give the stem a final layer of tape. If you want the tulip head to curve downward, shape the tulip head now, before the stem is beaded. (Photo 22)

8. Before adding the leaves, begin wrapping the stem with beads. Make certain that you have at least 9" of beads on the 26-gauge wire for every inch of stem wire that will be wrapped. *Note: The total length will depend on the length chosen for the final flower. The last 5" of stem wire will NOT be wrapped, so take this into consideration when calculating how many inches of beads you will need.*

   To wrap the stem, begin with 1" of bare wire at the base of the flower head. Wrap this wire once around the stem close to the tulip petals. Press the wire up against the stem and begin wrapping the beads very close to the flower bottom. (Photo 23)

9. Continue down the stem until reaching the point where you want the base of the first leaf to come out of the stem. At this point, stop wrapping. Temporarily, use a piece of masking tape to prevent the leaf from flopping around while you work. Secure the leaf, using floral tape, to the stem so the beads of the leaf are exactly beneath the last row you just wrapped on the stem. (Photo 24)

Photo 19

Photo 20

Photo 21

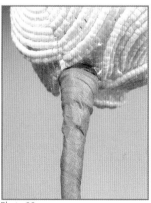

Photo 22

Photo 23

Photo 24

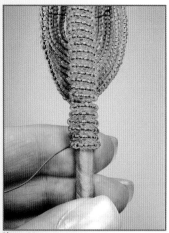
Photo 25

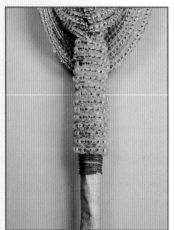
Photo 26

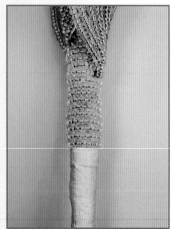
Photo 27

10. Continue bead wrapping the stem over the floral tape that is now holding the leaf. Make certain that all the rows continue to wrap tightly without any gaps. Wrap down to the point where you want to add the second leaf. (Photo 25)

11. Tape the second leaf to the stem. Use a piece of masking tape to temporarily hold the leaf while you finish bead wrapping the stem. Continue bead wrapping the stem.

12. End the wrapping approximately 3" from the bottom of the stem wire. To finish, wrap bare wire several times around the stem wire where the beads leave off. Try to get a smooth wrap with the wire to avoid having a ridge at the base of the beads. (Photo 26)

13. Continue taping down over the bare wire and down to the stem bottom. (Photo 27)

14. Remove masking tape from the leaves. Attach the leaves to the stem with short pieces of lacing wire, beginning at the lowest point on the highest leaf and working up the stem. Wrap the wire through the leaf and around the stem. Twist the wire tightly to hold the leaf in place. Trim excess wire. Do this in several places until the leaf holds the shape you desire. (Photo 28)

15. Wrap the lowest leaf completely around the stem and secure, using lacing wire. Trim the wire very close to the beads so the lacing wires do not show. Shape the leaf as desired. (Photo 29)

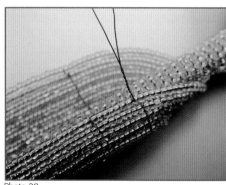
Photo 28

Photo 29

If you have completed the French Beaded Tulips, you may want to try these projects:

Tulip Tin on page 82
Clay Pot Critters on page 86

# French Beaded Anemones

**What You Need to Know:**

Round Basic on page 18
Pointed Basic on page 22
Continuous Loops on page 20
Lacing on page 26

Beehive Basic on page 36
Loopback Technique on page 37
Scalloped Edges on page 40

**What You Will Learn:**

Shaded Petals

## Materials (for Petals)

- Size 11° seed beads; or size 9° three-cut beads: dark color (1 hank)
- Size 11° seed beads; or size 9° three-cut beads: light color (1 hank)
- 26-gauge colored copper wire to match the light color beads (1 spool)
- 30-gauge colored copper wire to match the light color beads (optional) (1 spool)

## Materials (for Centers)

- Size 11° seed beads; or size 9° three-cut beads: black (1 hank)
- 26-gauge colored copper wire: black (1 spool)
- 30-gauge colored copper wire: black (optional) (1 spool)

## Materials (for Leaves)

- Size 11° seed beads; or size 9° three-cut beads: green (2 hanks)
- 24- or 26-gauge colored copper wire in coordinating color (1 spool)
- 30-gauge colored copper wire in coordinating color (1 spool)

## Other Supplies

- 18-gauge stem wire (3)
- 30-gauge paddle wire: green; or 28-gauge assembly wire: silver
- Floral tape: green

## Tools

- General Tools on page 12

## Making the Petals

**Pattern: Make 8**

**Basic ¾", 5 Rows, RTPB**
**Start scallops at Row 6. Make three scallops on each side**
**Shade petals with two colors**
**Trim so one long wire extends**
**Lace all petals, if desired**

1. Starting out with bare wire, place a knot in the end of the spool wire. Cut 40" of bare wire from the spool.

Photo 1

> **NOTE**
>
> *If using size 9° three-cut beads, cut 48" of bare wire. Because there is a discrepancy in the size of beads, it is better to be cautious and measure a little too much wire at first. After completing the first petal, you can determine how much extra wire you have at the end and reduce the number of inches of bare wire for subsequent petals. (Photo 1)*

2. String ¾" of dark beads for the basic and add one light bead. The basic wire only needs to be 1" at the top. Make the loop of the basic frame 4" long. Twist the loop 2" beneath the basic beads.

3. Create an inverted "V" with the light-colored beads. Add two light beads followed by as many dark beads as necessary to complete the first row. Make the top round. Make the next row, adding enough dark beads to complete the row. Remove the last three beads and replace with light beads. Make the bottom pointed.

4. Continue with Rows 4 and 5 in the same manner, starting and finishing each row with the number of light beads necessary to create the inverted "V." (Photo 2)

5. Begin making scallops in the Row 6. Start the first scallop five beads from the petal top. Be certain to shade properly as you make each scallop. Make the bottom pointed. Make three scallops on each side. Each scallop is five beads from the previous scallop. If desired, lace each petal. (Photo 3)

Photo 2

## Making the Center

**Patterns: Make 1**  **Basic 3, 10 Rows, RTRB**
**Make a beehive**

**Make 2**  **10–12 continuous loops, 12 beads in each loop**

Photo 3

### NOTE

*The center consists of two parts. The first part is a beehive center consisting of 10 rows. The second part of the center is a series of continuous loops.*

1. String 10" of black beads on the wire. After the first two rows, bend the top and bottom basic wires as shown in the photo. Continue beading around the basic frame, making the top and bottom round. When 10 rows have been completed, you will be at the top basic wire. Twist the spool wire and the top basic wire together to form one stem wire. Cut the wire from the spool. Open the loop at the bottom and twist the wires together to form the other stem wire. (Photo 4)

Photo 4

2. String 12" of black beads on the wire. Make enough 12-bead loops to fit around the beehive. Determine the number of continuous loops that are necessary to fit around the beehive by holding one tail wire next to one of the beehive stem wires. Make enough loops so that the last loop reaches the second beehive stem wire. You will need between 10 and 12 loops to fit around the beehive. Make the second series of continuous loops to fit around the remaining side of the beehive. (Photo 5)

3. Assemble the center as follows:

   **a.** Start with the first series of continuous loops. Wrap the tail wire around the first beehive stem wire. Wrap the end tail wire around the

Photo 5

Photo 6

Photo 7

Photo 8

remaining beehive stem wire. Wrap the tail wire of the second series of continuous loops around one of the beehive stem wires. Finish by closing the circle of loops around the beehive. Wrap the end tail wire of the loops around the remaining beehive stem wire. (Photo 6)

**b.** If there are any gaps between the loops and the beehive, correct by pulling the loops close to the beehive with lacing wire. Simply cut a piece of lacing wire and wrap through the bottom row of the beehive and around the loops. Secure the lacing wire and trim the excess. (Photo 7)

**c.** Press the loops so they stand straight up against the beehive. Bend both stem wires to meet underneath the beehive. Twist the stem wires together to form one stem. (Photo 8)

## Making the Leaves

**Patterns: Make 1**      **Basic 2½", 5 Rows, PTPB**
                          **After the fifth row, make three loops on each side, using the loopback technique**
                          **Use 6" of green beads for Loop 1 and 2**
                          **Use 5" of green beads for Loop 3 and 4**
                          **Use 4" of green beads for Loop 5 and 6**
                          **Trim so three wires extend**

**Make 3**      **Basic 1½", 5 Rows, PTPB**
               **After the fifth row make three loops on each side, using the loopback technique**
               **Use 4½" of green beads for Loops 1 and 2**
               **Use 3½" of green beads for Loops 3 and 4**
               **Use 2½" of green beads for Loops 5 and 6**
               **Trim so three wires extend**

1. Keep the bottom pointed. (Photo 9)

2. Lace each leaf in two places. Lace the center across the first five rows, then lace the bottom across all rows. Starting at the bottom of the basic row, lace across all rows including the loops. Angle the lacing to make an inverted "V" in order to catch all the loops in the lacing. (Photo 10)

Photo 9

Photo 10

## Assembling the Anemones

1. Tape the three stem wires individually. Tape the three pieces together to form one stem.

2. Attach the center to the top of the stem wire, using 28-gauge, assembly wire, or 30-gauge, paddle wire. Keep the wire just below the center. (Photo 11)

3. Attach each petal, one at a time, with assembly wire. Place the good side of the petal facing up. Wrap each petal approximately three times with the assembly wire to secure. (Photo 12)

4. Attach the first four petals, one on each side of the center. (Photo 13)

5. After the first four petals have been attached, cut the assembly wire and tape down the stem, using floral tape. Cover the assembly wire with the tape. *Note: It is not necessary to tape the entire length of the stem.* (Photo 14)

6. Attach the remaining petals underneath the first four petals, one at a time as before, in the spaces that were created by the first four petals. These petals also face upward. (Photo 15)

7. After all the petals have been attached, wrap the assembly wire around the stem approximately ¼" below the petals. Cut the assembly wire from the spool. (Photo 16)

Photo 11

Photo 12

Photo 13

Photo 14

Photo 15

Photo 16

Photo 17

Photo 18

Photo 19

8. Trim all the petal wires by staggering the lengths of the wires. (Photo 17)

9. Tape over the assembly wires and continue down the entire stem length. (Photo 18)

10. Bend the stem wire slightly so the flower head gently curves. Shape the petals by cupping them around the center. To make the flower look more realistic, make certain that you do not cup each petal exactly the same way. (Photo 19)

11. Secure the leaves, one at a time, with floral tape. Place the stem wire of the leaf flat against the flower stem. Do not allow any leaf stem wire to show. Place the first leaf approximately 3" below the head of the flower. (Photo 20) The leaves of an Anemone form a collar around the stem.

12. Tape the remaining leaves, one at a time, at the same level as the first leaf so they circle the flower stem. Bend the leaves in all directions to make them look wild with a fringed appearance. (Photo 21)

Photo 20

Photo 21

If you have completed the French Beaded Anemones, you may want to try this project:

Towel Rack on page 97

# French Beaded Hydrangeas

**What You Need to Know:**
Round Basic on page 18
Pointed Basic on page 22
Continuous Loops on page 20
Scallop Edges on page 40
Shaded Petals on page 37

**What You Will Learn:**
Continuous Double Loops
Continuous Triple Loops
Continuous Quadruple Loops

## Materials (for Petals)

- Size 11° seed beads; or size 9° three-cut beads: dark color (3 hanks)
- Size 11° seed beads; or size 9° three-cut beads: light color (2 hanks)
- 26-gauge colored copper wire in coordinating color (47 yds)

## Materials (for Centers)

- Size 8° seed beads: light green or pale yellow (104)

## Materials (for Leaves)

- Size 11° seed beads; or size 9° three-cut beads: green (2 hanks)
- 24-gauge colored copper wire: green (9 yds)
- 30-gauge colored copper wire: green

## Other Supplies

- 18-gauge stem wire (11)
- Floral tape: green

## Tools

- General Tools on page 12

## Making the Petals

**Pattern: Make 8 bunches**
        **Make 5**

**Make 1 bunch as follows:**
**4 continuous single loops with 9 beads in each loop**

1. Measure and cut 10" piece from 26-gauge wire.

2. Shade petals for each loop, using the following pattern: three light beads, three dark beads, three light beads. Leave a 4" tail at the beginning and make four continuous loops as close together as possible. Leave a 4" tail at the end. (Photo 1)

3. Add the flower center by bringing one tail wire up through to the flower top. Place one size 8° bead on the wire. (Photo 2)

Photo 1

Photo 2

Photo 3

4. Bring the wire down to the flower bottom and twist the two tail wires together down the length of the wires to form the stem. (Photo 3)

**Pattern: Make 3**
**4 continuous loops:**
**Start with one triple loop followed by three double loops, starting each loop with seven beads**

1. Cut 15" from bare wire. Start with the triple loop. Start all loops with seven beads. Leave a 4" tail at the beginning and end of every flower. The color pattern of the first loop is as follows: two light beads, three dark beads, two light beads. (Photo 4)

2. Start the second row with three light beads. Add enough dark beads to go completely around the first loop. (Photo 5)

3. After you have just enough dark beads to close the circle, remove the last three beads and replace them with three light beads. Twist the loop two half turns to secure. (Photo 6)

4. Start the third row with five light beads followed by enough dark beads to go all the way around the second loop. (Photo 7)

5. When you have enough beads to close the loop, remove the last five dark beads and replace them with five light beads. Twist the loop two half turns to secure. (Photo 8)

6. Follow the triple loop with three double loops. Start the first double loop ⅛" from the triple loop to allow enough room for the second row. Begin each double loop with seven beads. Follow the same color pattern for the double loop that you used to create the first two rows of the triple loop. When the second row is completed, twist the loops two half turns to secure. (Photos 9 & 10)

Photo 4

Photo 5

Photo 8

Photo 9

Photo 10

Photo 6

7. After three double loops are completed, create the center with one size 8° seed bead in the same manner as the continuous single loop flowers. Refer to Steps 3–4 on page 53. (Photo 11)

Photo 11

Photo 7

Photo 12

Photo 13

Photo 14

Photo 15

**Pattern: Make 5**

**4 continuous loops:
Start with one quadruple loop, followed by three triple loops, starting each loop with seven beads**

1. Cut 23" of bare wire. Start the flower in the same manner as the triple loop. Make it a quadruple loop, adding seven light beads followed by enough dark beads to close the circle. When the circle is complete, remove the last seven dark beads and replace them with seven light beads. Twist the loop four half turns to secure. This will prevent the rows from separating as you work with the next three continuous loops. (Photo 12)

2. Follow the quadruple loop with three continuous triple loops. Start the first triple loop ¼" from the quadruple loop to allow enough room for the three rows. Begin each triple loop with seven beads. Complete three triple loops. (Photos 13 & 14)

3. After you have completed three triple loops, add the center and finish the flower in the same manner as the other flowers. (Photo 15)

4. Repeat the patterns to make a total of 8 bunches. *Note: Each bunch will contain 13 flowers.*

## Making the Leaves

**Pattern: Make 3**

**Basic 1", 7 Rows, RBPT, followed by 10 scallops on each side
Trim so three long wires extend**

*Note: When creating the basic, leave a 1" top basic wire. Make a large enough loop so that you can twist the wire together for 2" and still have a loop that is 2" long.*

1. String 11" of green beads on the wire. Make the first seven rows RBPT. After the seventh row, cut 80" of bare wire to make the scallops.

2. Make the first nine scallops on each side, seven beads from the previous scallop. The first scallop is seven beads from the leaf point.

3. Make the tenth scallop on each side, half the length of the row before it. (Photo 16)

Photo 16

> **NOTE**
>
> *When you make each scallop, it is important to make each scallop seven beads from the previous scallop on average. This means that if you make one scallop six beads, another seven beads, and another eight beads, the leaf will turn out well. (Photo 17)*

Notice the differences that occur when you change the number of beads consistently. The center leaf (Photo 18) has eight beads between every scallop. The leaf is longer and narrower. The leaf on the right (Photo 19) has six beads between every scallop. This leaf is wider and there wasn't enough wire to complete all 10 scallops. (Photo 19)

Photo 17

Photo 18

Photo 19

The reason one bead can make such a difference is that in total you are making 20 scallops. Twenty beads are a little over 1". Multiply this effect by the length of the rows and you can see how it will make a difference in the 80" of bare wire that you started with. That is the only reason that you need to watch the number of beads in each scallop. Certainly, Mother Nature is not exact and any given hydrangea plant would have multitudes of different size leaves. If different sized and shaped leaves are desired, adjust the length of bare wire that you work with before starting to make the scallops.

4. Tape one stem wire. Place the stem wire on the leaf so the top of stem begins at the bottom of the basic beads. Tape the wire down the entire stem. (Photo 20)

5. Attach the support wire to the leaf with a piece of lacing wire. Begin by passing the lacing wire from the leaf front to the back, and crossing the wires in the back. Pass the lacing wire to the front, cross the wires, and return to the back. Continue down the leaf length. (Photo 21)

Photo 20

Photo 21

French Beaded Hydrangeas  57

Photo 22

6. At the leaf bottom, twist the two wires together on the back side and trim close to the stem wire. This will strengthen this large leaf. (Photo 22)

## Assembling the Hydrangea

1. Each of the eight bunches contains 13 flowers. Separate each bunch into into three flower groups as follows: 1) the five continuous loop flowers (Photo 23), 2) the three triple loop flowers plus one quadruple loop flower (Photo 24), and 3) the remaining four quadruple loop flowers. Tape each flower with half the width of the floral tape. (Photo 25)

Photo 23

Photo 24

Photo 25

Photo 26

2. Tape each of the flowers within a group together, letting approximately 1½"–2" of flower stem showing. Keep the stems as flat as possible when taping. To do this, place them next to each other and squeeze flat when you wrap.

3. Repeat for the remaining groups.

4. Tape eight stem wires individually. Attach the three groups in one bunch to one stem wire as follows:

   a. Start with Group 1. Tape the top of the stem wire at the base of the flower group. Keep the tape at this level. (Photo 26)

**b.** Secure Group 2 and Group 3, one at a time, using the floral tape. Using the flat sides of the second and third groups, make a triangle around the stem wire. Tape half way down the stem wire. (Photo 27)

**c.** Repeat for the remaining seven.

5. Tape three bunches together as shown, fanning out the flowers on top. Keep the floral tape at this level. (Photo 28)

6. Secure two more bunches, one on each side of the three bunches taped together. If desired, place these at a lower level than the first three. Position as desired. Some people prefer rounder hydrangea balls and some people prefer them to be a little flatter. To create a rounder ball, place these two bunches at a lower level than the first three bunches. (Photo 29)

**TIP**

*When making an arrangement of hydrangeas, vary the shape of each hydrangea to make it look as if you picked them from the garden.*

Photo 27

Photo 28

Photo 29

7. Secure the remaining three bunches so the flower takes on the shape that you desire. (Photo 30)

Photo 30

Photo 31

8. Continue taping down the entire stem length. (Photo 31)

9. Add three leaves, one at a time, using floral tape.

10. When all three leaves have been added, tape down the entire length of the stem. (Photo 32)

11. Shape the flowers and the leaves as desired.

### TIP

*In an arrangement it is often better not to attach the leaves to the stem of the flower. Simply insert them into the container to fill any open spaces between the flowers.*

If you have completed the French Beaded Hydrangeas, you may want to try this project:

Lamp Shade on page 97

Photo 32

When shaping the leaves and flowers, keep in mind the container, which will hold the french beaded hydrangeas. Once the flowers have been placed in the desired container, take a step back and view the arrangement as a whole, then reshape flowers and leaves as necessary.

# Projects

NAPKIN RING

ROSE TOPIARY

BLACK TIE CANDLEHOLDERS

FORSYTHIA URN

TULIP TIN

CLAY POT CRITTERS

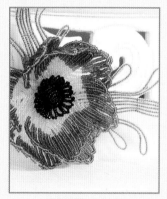

TOWEL RACK

LAMP SHADE

FALL BERRY WREATH

WHEAT VOTIVES

MISTLETOE BALL

CHRISTMAS TREE

# Napkin Ring

What You Need to Know:

French Beaded Wildflowers on page 16

## Materials (for one Napkin Ring)

- 18" length of 26-gauge colored copper wire in coordinating color with size 6° seed beads (3)
- Size 6° seed beads: multicolored (108)
- Screen-box clasp
- Three-hole spacer bars (2)
- Wildflower with variations noted below

## Tools

- General Tools on page 12
- Flat-nosed pliers

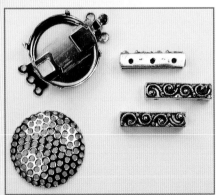

The napkin ring will be created on a screen-box clasp. You will need three-hole spacer bars for the ring.

## Making the Wildflower

1. Using 26-gauge wire, make all the parts of a Wildflower as follows:

   **a.** Make one extra petal for a total of six petals. (Photo 1)

   **b.** Make center with five loops. (Photo 2)

Photo 1

Photo 2

   **c.** Make center with two loops. (Photo 3)

   **d.** Make calyx with 12 continuous loops, with the same color beads as used on the center five loops. (Photo 4)

Photo 3

Photo 4

**e.** Do not make leaves.

**f.** Do not assemble the wildflower.

2. Remove and discard the clasps from both sides of the screen-box clasp. (Photo 5)

Photo 5

## Assembling the Napkin Ring

1. Twist the tail wires of the five-loop center together to form one stem wire. Twist all the way to the end and trim the wires even. Insert the stem wire into a hole in the screen near the screen center. Pull the wire through so the beads touch the screen. (Photo 6)

2. Twist the tail wires of the two-loop center together to form one stem wire. Insert this stem directly into a hole in the center of the five loops and the screen and pull through so the beads touch the screen. (Photo 7)

3. Curve the five loops up away from the screen so it is easier to attach the petals. Insert the stem of the first petal into a hole in the screen close to the five-loop center and pull through so the beads touch the screen. *Note: The petals will be a little floppy until all six petals are added and the wires are twisted underneath.* (Photo 8)

4. Attach the remaining petals, one at a time. Insert each stem in a hole so the petal overlaps the one next to it. Continue around the circle until all six petals have been added. (Photo 9)

Photo 9

Photo 6

Photo 7

Photo 8

5. After all six petals have been added and using flat-nosed pliers, tightly twist all the wires beneath the screen together into one thick stem. (Photo 10)

6. Using flat-nosed pliers, press the twisted wires flat against the screen. Trim the wires so only ¼" remains under the screen. (Photo 11)

7. Wrap the calyx around the petals on top of the screen, but beneath the petals. Close the circle. Twist the two tail wires together. Insert the tail wires into a hole in the screen. Press the wire against the screen and cut it so only ¼" remains under the screen. Set the flower aside. (Photo 12)

8. Run one 18" wire through both ends of the box clasp. (Photo 13)

9. Add 12 size 6° seed beads to each wire end followed by one spacer bar, then followed by six more size 6° seed beads. Tie a knot in each wire end. (Photo 14)

Photo 10

Photo 14

Photo 11

10. Run a second 18" wire through both ends of the box clasp. To each of these ends add 12 beads, pass the wire through the second hole in the spacer bar, and add six more beads. Tie a knot in each end of the wire. (Photo 15)

Photo 15

Photo 12

## TIP

*If you are using decorative spacer bars, be certain the decorative side faces up on both sides of the box clasp.*

Photo 13

Photo 18

Photo 19

Photo 20

Photo 21

11. Repeat Step 10 on page 65 for the third 18" wire. Pass the wire through the third hole in the spacer bar. Tie a knot in each wire end. (Photo 16)

Photo 16

12. Remove the knots from both ends of the first wire. Working with the clasp on the bottom, pass the wire end on the left through the six beads on the wire on the right. Pass the wire end on the right through the six beads on the wire on the left. Pull both wires very taut, creating a circle with the beads. Try to pull the wires taut enough so that there are no gaps between any beads in the circle. (Photo 17)

Photo 17

13. On one side, bring the wire underneath the spacer bar. Wrap the wire on the other side of the spacer bar between the spacer and the next bead. Wrap four or five times to secure the beads. Trim the wire very close to the beads. Repeat on the remaining side. (Photo 18)

14. Repeat Steps 12 and 13 above for the two remaining rows of beads. When all three rows have been wrapped and the wires trimmed, the ring is ready for the flower. (Photo 19)

15. Place the screen on top of the clasp. Using flat-nosed pliers, crimp the four prongs over the top of the screen. (Photo 20)

16. Crimping the prongs may have caused the shape of the ring to become distorted or flattened some of the flower petals. Reshape the flowers so that the petals curve up and the calyx curves down. Press the beads of the ring into a circular shape. (Photo 21)

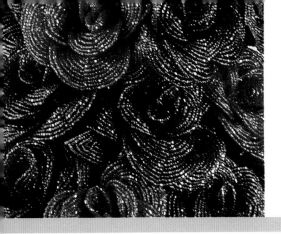

# Rose Topiary

**What You Need to Know:**
French Beaded Roses on page 26

## Materials

- Roses with variations noted on page 69 (44)
- Rose leaves with variations noted on page 70 (24)
- Pillar candleholder*; or 6" dia. cake stand
- Cone-shaped foam topiary form, 4" x 12"
- Acrylic paint: forest green (2 oz.)
- Nonhardening clay (small lump)
- 6" wooden skewer

## Tools

- General Tools on page 12
- Paintbrush

*I like the candleholder because it has a cup for the candle, which I can fill with nonhardening clay to help support the topiary form.*

## NOTE

*If necessary, prepare the candleholder. I found these pillar candleholders with beaded decorations in a discount store. I decided that it would make a great stand for the topiary, but I didn't want the beads. So, I simply cut them off and saved them for another use. (Photo 1)*

Photo 1

## Preparing the Topiary Form

1. Paint the topiary form with green paint to hide any spaces that may appear around the roses. (Photo 2)

2. Set up the topiary stand. Insert a wooden skewer into the bottom of the topiary form at the center point. Leave enough skewer sticking out that will fit into the candleholder indentation. (Photo 3)

Photo 2

Photo 3

3. Fill the indentation with the clay and insert the skewer into the center of the clay. Push the form down so it is flush with the candleholder top. (Photo 4)

Photo 4

**NOTE**

*If using a cake stand, cut an indentation in the bottom of the topiary form so the lump of clay will fit inside it. When the form sits on top of the cake stand, be certain the bottom of the form is flush with the top of the cake stand. Place the lump of clay in the center of the stand, insert the skewer into the lump of clay, and press the form down so that it is flush with the top of the cake stand.*

## Making the Roses

1. Make roses as follows:

   **a.** Make 16 roses with garnet, size 9° three-cut beads. Make each rose on one piece of 16-gauge wire. Cut the stem wire to 4". Do not curve the top of the roses on the stem wire. Make the sepals for the roses, but do not make the branches of leaves.

   **b.** Make 16 roses with ruby, size 9° three-cut beads. Make each rose on one piece of 16-gauge wire. Cut the stem wire to 4". Do not curve the top of the roses on the stem wire. Make the sepals for the roses, but do not make the branches of leaves.

   **c.** Make six rosebuds with garnet, size 9° three-cut beads. Make each rosebud on one piece of 16-gauge wire. Cut the stem wire to 4". Do not curve the top of the rosebuds on the wire. Make the sepals for the rosebuds, but do not make the branches of leaves.

Photo 5

   **d.** Make six rosebuds with ruby, size 9° three-cut beads. Make each rosebud on one piece of 16- gauge wire. Cut the wire to 4". Do not curve the top of the rosebuds on the wire. Make the sepals for the rosebuds, but do not make the branches of leaves.

   **e.** To make one rosebud, use only the five largest petals. Refer to **Making the Last Five Petals**, Steps 1–3 on pages 29–30. Take one petal and roll it to form the center of the rosebud. Add the remaining petals and the sepals to form the complete rosebud. (Photos 5 & 6)

   **NOTE**

   *Making a bud with the largest petals, rather than the smaller inner petals will result in a rosebud that more realistically resembles the flower just before the petals begin to open.*

Photo 6

Photo 7

Photo 8

Completed roses and rosebuds before being inserted into the topiary.

2. Insert the roses into the topiary form. Start at the bottom of the form. Place the roses close together to minimize the spaces. Alternate the colors between the garnet and the ruby roses. If necessary, trim the stem wires before inserting them into the form. *Note: As you move up the topiary form, the cone is less than 4" in diameter. It will then be necessary to trim the stems to avoid having them pierce through the other side of the cone.* (Photo 7)

3. Continue adding roses row by row, moving up the cone. Intersperse some buds in between the full roses. Save five buds for the very top of the topiary. At the top, place one bud at the center of the cone. Place the remaining four buds on alternate sides just below the center bud. (Photo 8)

## Making the Leaves

**Pattern: Make 24**      **Basic 6, 15 rows, RBPT**
**Trim so three long wires extend**
**Lace all leaves**

## Finishing the Topiary

1. Insert the leaves into the spaces between the roses and the buds. Use as many or as few leaves as desired. (Photo 9)

2. Press the stems into the topiary so only the leaf tips are seen through the roses.

Photo 9

# Black Tie Candleholders

**What You Need to Know:**
French Beaded Wildflowers on page 71
French Beaded Daisies on page 34

## Materials (for one Flower)

- Size 9° three-cut beads: white (1 strand)
- Size 9° three-cut beads: black (4 strands)
- 26-gauge colored copper wire: black (3 yds)
- 26-gauge colored copper wire: white or silver (1 yd)
- 1.8 cm dia. screen with back

## Other Supplies

- Candleholders with holes (2)

## Tools

- General Tools on page 12
- Flat-nosed pliers

*Note: Make enough flowers for the number of holes in the candleholders. I purchased my candleholders from a discount store, on the clearance table. They already came with holes drilled in them. A few of the holes had some split rings, which I removed.*

This photo shows the five flower layers.

## Making the Flowers

**Pattern for the First Layer:**
Make 1 in black    12 continuous 1½" loops
Leave a 3" tail at each end
Twist the two tail wires together to form one stem

**Pattern for the Second Layer:**
Make 1 in black    12 continuous 2" 4-row crossover loops
Leave a 3" tail at each end
Twist the two tail wires together to form one stem

**Pattern for the Third Layer:**
Make 1 in white    10 continuous 1" loops
Leave a 3" tail at each end
Twist the two tail wires together to form one stem

**Pattern for the Fourth Layer:**
Make 1 in white    5 continuous 10-bead loops
Leave a 3" tail at each end
Twist the two tail wires together to form one stem

**Pattern for the Fifth Layer:**
Make 1 in black    2 continuous 8-bead loops
Leave a 3" tail at each end
Twist the two tail wires together to form one stem

Photo 1

Photo 2

Photo 3

## Assembling the Candleholders

1. Assemble the flowers on a small metal screen. *Note: The wires will get covered by the back of the screen so they cannot be seen as the flowers circle around the candleholders. The first flower layer is the only layer that will not pass through the screen. The wire that extends from the circle of loops will be used to attach the finished flower to the candleholder.* (Photo 1)

2. Lay the first layer on center front of the screen. (Photo 2)

3. Insert the stem of the second layer into the circle of the first layer. Push the stem through a hole in the screen. Choose a hole that is close to the edge of the circle of the first layer, keeping the center of the screen free for the next layers. (Photo 3)

4. Insert the stem of the third layer into a hole in the screen. Choose a hole that is on the opposite side of the stem from the second layer, and is near the edge of the circle of the second layer. (Photo 4)

5. Insert the stem of the fourth layer into the screen. Choose a hole that is on the opposite side of the stem from the third layer, and is near the edge of the circle of the third layer. (Photo 5)

6. Insert the stem of the fifth layer into the center of the screen. (Photo 6)

7. Turn the screen over to the back side and twist the four wires together. Remember, the first layer was on front of the screen, not through it. Using nylon pliers, twist the wires very tightly. Using flat-nosed pliers, flatten the wires against the screen. (Photo 7)

Photo 4

Photo 5

Photo 6

Photo 7

Photo 9

Photo 10

Photo 11

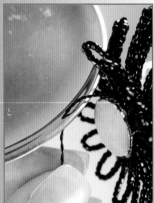

Photo 8

8. Cut the wires to ¼". Press wires flat inside the screen. (Photo 8)

9. Place the back on the screen. Using the flat-nosed pliers, crimp the prongs over the screen. *Note: This may flatten out the petals on the front. You can fix this after the backing has been crimped.* (Photo 9)

10. Shape the petals on the front. Curve the first layer toward the back of the flower. Curve remaining layers toward the front. (Photo 10)

11. Prepare the candleholders, if necessary. *Note: The candleholders used in this project already came with drilled holes.* (Photo 11)

12. Insert the wire from the first layer into the top of one of the holes in the candleholder. Insert the wire from the top, down so that the flower will hang properly. (Photo 12)

13. Pull the flower very close to the candleholder and wrap the stem wire around itself four or five times to secure the flower. When the flower is secure, trim the stem wire close underneath the flower. (Photo 13)

14. Continue adding the remaining flowers to the candleholder. (Photo 14)

Photo 12

Photo 13

Photo 14

# Forsythia Urn

**What You Need to Know:**
Continuous Loops on page 20
Continuous 4-row Crossover Loops on page 34

## Materials (for one 30" Branch)

- Size 8° seed beads: yellow (24)
- Size 9° three-cut beads; or size 11° seed beads: dark brown (1 strand)
- Size 9° three-cut beads; or size 11° seed beads: very pale transparent green (4 strands)
- Size 9° three-cut beads; or size 11° seed beads: yellow (2 hanks)
- 26-gauge colored copper wire: brown (2 yds)
- 26-gauge colored copper wire: gold (15 yds)
- 28-gauge colored copper wire: gold (10 yds)

## Other Supplies

- 16-gauge stem wire (3)
- 18-gauge stem wire (3)
- Floral tape: brown

## Materials (for 65 Branches of Blooms)

- Size 8° seed beads: yellow (1,560)
- Size 9° three-cut beads; or size 11° seed beads: dark brown (6 hanks)
- Size 9° three-cut beads; or size 11° seed beads: very pale transparent green (25 hanks)

- Size 9° three-cut beads; or size 11° seed beads: yellow (11 half-kilo bags)
- 26-gauge colored copper wire: brown (130 yds)
- 26-gauge colored copper wire: gold (975 yds)
- 28-gauge colored copper wire: gold (650 yds)

## Other Supplies

- 16-gauge stem wire (173 pieces)
- 18-gauge stem wire (63 pieces)
- 12"–15" tall metal urn*
- Floral tape: brown (15 rolls)
- Nonhardening clay to fill the urn (approximately 14 lbs.)

## Tools

- General Tools on page 12

> **NOTE**
> *A half-kilo bag of size 9° three-cut beads will make six branches.*

*I recommend using a metal urn. In my first attempt to assemble the arrangement, I used a porcelain urn and it cracked from the weight of the clay and the heavy branches.*

## Making the Blossoms

**Pattern: Make 4**     **4 continuous ¾" loops**

1. String at least 4" of yellow beads on the 26-gauge, gold wire. Leave a 3" tail at each end. Twist the tail wires together to form one stem wire. Press the loops together to form a bud. Set aside. (Photo 1)

Photo 1

Photo 2

Photo 3

Photo 4

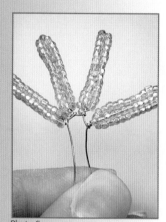

Photo 5

Photo 6

Photo 7

**Pattern: Make 8        4 continuous 1¼" loops**

1. String at least 5" of yellow beads on the 26-gauge gold wire. Leave a 3" tail at each end. It is important to make each loop ⅛" from the previous loop. Continue until you have four continuous loops. (Photo 2)

2. Twist the tail wires together to form one stem wire. *Note: You will have a small hole in the center of the blossom. It is important to twist the tail wires together so you leave a hole in the center. This is where you will insert the center bead. If you do not insert the center bead into the hole it will fall out of the flower as you assemble it.* (Photo 3)

3. Shape the blossom by cupping the petals up, then arching the tips over. Keep the loops long and narrow. (Photo 4)

**Pattern: Make 16        4 continuous 1½" 4-row crossover loops**

1. String at least 12" of yellow of beads on the 26-gauge gold wire. Leave a 3" tail at each end. Make a total of four continuous 4-row crossover loops. Be certain to leave the same ⅛" of bare wire in between each loop as for the other blossoms. (Photo 5)

2. Twist the tail wires together to form one stem wire. There will be a small hole in the center of the loops. (Photo 6)

3. Shape the blossom by cupping the petals up, then arching the tips over. Keep the crossover loops long and tubular. Do not let them flatten out. (Photo 7)

## Making the Centers

**Pattern: Make 24    Single bead stamens with size 8° seed beads**

1. Cut 6" from the 28-gauge gold wire. Place one size 8° seed bead in the wire center and fold the wire in half. Twist the wire ends together to form one stem. Twist directly under the bead, to the ends of the wire. Trim the wire ends to the same length, making it easier to insert into the center hole of the blossom. (Photo 8)

2. Insert one center into each of the 1¼" blossoms and one center into each of the 1½" blossoms. Twist the stem wires together to form one stem. Set aside. (Photo 9)

## Making the Sepals

**Pattern: Make 4    2 continuous 8-bead loops**

1. Begin with 16 brown beads on the 26-gauge brown wire. Leave a 3" tail at each end. Make two 8-bead loops. Make the loops in the same manner that you made the blossoms. Twist the two tail wires together to form one stem wire. Press the two loops together. (Photo 10)

**Pattern: Make 4    4 continuous 6-bead loops**

1. String 24 brown beads on the 26-gauge, brown wire. Leave a 3" tail at the beginning and at the end. Make a total of four 6-bead loops in the same manner as the blossoms. Twist the tail wires together to form one stem wire. *Note: There will be a small hole in the center of the loops.* (Photo 11)

2. Insert a ¾" blossom into the center of the 6-bead sepals. Twist the two stem wires together to form one stem. Set aside. (Photo 12)

Photo 8

Photo 9

Photo 10

Photo 11

Photo 12

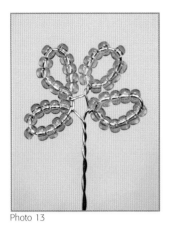

Photo 13

Photo 14

Photo 15

Photo 16

**Pattern: Make 8      4 continuous ½" loops**

1. String 2" of green beads on the 28-gauge, gold wire. Leave a 3" tail at each end. Make a total of four ½" loops in the same manner as you made the blossoms. Twist the two tail wires together to form one stem wire. *Note: There will be a small hole in the center of the loops.* (Photo 13)

2. Insert 1¼" blossom into the center of the ½" sepals. Twist the two stem wires together to form one stem wire. Set aside. (Photo 14)

**Pattern: Make 16      4 continuous ¾" loops**

1. String 4" of green beads on the 28-gauge gold wire. Leave a 3" tail at each end. Make a total of four ¾" loops in the same manner as the blossoms. Twist the tail wires together to form one stem wire. *Note: There will be a small hole in the center of the loops.* (Photo 15)

2. Insert a 4-row crossover blossom into the center of the ¾" sepals. Twist the stem wires together to form one stem wire. Set aside. (Photo 16)

# Making One 30" Branch

1. Tape three 18-gauge stem wires and three 16-gauge stem wires individually with brown floral tape.

2. Make Section "A" as follows:

   **a.** Cut off 6" each from two 18-gauge stem wires. Set the 6" pieces aside. Line up the bottoms of one 18" and two 12" pieces of 18-gauge stems. Tape the stems together along the entire length for a "tapered" stem.

3. Make Section "B" as follows:

   **a.** Cut off 6" each from two 16-gauge stem wires. *Note: You should now have a total of five 16-gauge pieces in different lengths.*

   **b.** Line up the bottoms of all five pieces and tape them together along the entire length. *Note: You will have a stem that has three different thicknesses with the thinnest part at the top.*

Photo 17

Photo 18

Photo 19

Photo 20

4. Tape Section B to Section A by overlapping the portion of Section B that is the thinnest with the bottom of Section A. Tape the entire length of the stem. You should now have a branch that is approximately 30" long and varies from thin to thick from top to bottom.

5. Attach the 6" pieces, which were set aside from Section A, as desired along the branch. *Note: Do not worry about any bumps that resulted from taping the different lengths of wire. They will make the branch look more natural.* (Photo 17)

## Assembling the Branch

1. Set the branch down on the table and place the buds and blossoms in random order along the branch so you can see where you would like to attach them. When arranged as desired, pick up the branch and begin attaching the blossoms from the top to the bottom.

2. Using half the thickness of the brown floral tape, attach the first blossom to the tip of the branch. *Note: It does not matter what size you choose. Each branch should be different. Attach the blossom so that there is no stem wire showing between the branch and the sepals.* Cover the wire with 1" of brown floral tape. Trim the stem of the blossom. (Photo 18)

3. Position the four brown sepal loops throughout the branch. Place the buds and blossoms on all sides of the branch. *Note: The little brown bumps on the branch will look like a new bud is forming.* (Photo 19)

4. Continue adding the blossoms, keeping some close together and spreading others farther apart until they are all attached. (Photo 20)

## Making the Additional Branches for the Urn

1. Make the flowers for all 65 branches.

2. Cut and assemble the stem wires for branches as follows:

   **a.** Make twenty-one 30" branches consisting of one Section A and one Section B as described in Steps 1–5 on page 79 and above.

   **b.** Make twenty-two 24" branches consisting of one Section B plus one 12" piece of 16-gauge, wire. Tape the piece of 16-gauge, stem wire. Attach the 12" piece to the top of Section B overlapping the top 6" of Section B with the bottom 6" of 12" piece of stem wire. Set aside the 6" pieces to attach to the branches later.

   **c.** Make eleven 18" branches. Tape eleven pieces of 16-gauge stem wire individually.

   **d.** Make eleven 12" branches. Tape eleven pieces of 16-gauge stem wire individually. Cut to 12" length, setting aside the 6" pieces to attach to the branches later.

3. Attach all the flowers to the branches, starting with the 12" branches and working up to the longer branches. *Note: Any flowers that do not fit on the shorter branches can be used on the extra 6" lengths of wire and attached to the longer branches when you get to them.*

## Filling the Urn

1. Fill the urn to the top with nonhardening clay.

2. Insert the 30" branches in the back of the urn, starting in the middle and working out to the sides. Place the stems in the middle vertically while placing the stems out to the sides at a slight angle. Set aside five 30" branches. (Photo 21)

3. Add the 24" branches in front of the 30" branches. Fill in the spaces, keeping to the fan shape. Set aside five 24" branches. (Photo 22)

4. Add the 18" branches near the front of the urn. Fill in where needed. Make certain to angle some of these branches to the front of the urn, making a semicircle in addition to keeping the shape of the fan.

5. Fill in the open spaces with the 12" branches. (Photo 23)

6. Shape the branches so that some curve and bend the way real forsythia branches curve and bend. Add the remaining 30" branches and the remaining 24" branches wherever necessary. (Photo 24)

Photo 21

Photo 22

Photo 23

Photo 24

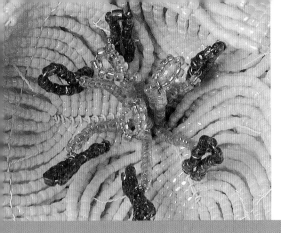

# Tulip Tin

**What You Need to Know:**
French Beaded Tulips on page 40

## Materials

- Tulips with variations noted below (12)
- Size 11° seed beads for handle (2 hanks)
- 28-gauge colored copper wire for handle
- 30-gauge colored copper wire: green
- 6" lengths of 16-gauge stem wire (24)
- Floral tapes: green; coordinating color for handle
- Flower tin for door*
- Nonhardening clay (5 lbs.)

## Tools

- General Tools on page 12

*Purchase a tin with a very sturdy handle. When the tin is filled with the clay and the tulips, it is very heavy.*

## Making the Tulips

1. Make 12 tulips with the following variations:

   **a.** Make two leaves for each flower, but do not attach them to the stem of the flower.

   **b.** Curve the stems of the tulips so that five tulips are very curved, four tulips have a medium curve, and three tulips have a slight curve. Bead the stems of each tulip 12".

   **c.** Tape the 24 stem wires with green floral tape.

   **d.** Attach one stem wire to each leaf. Place the stem at the bottom of the basic beads and secure in a few places, using 30-gauge wire. Tape the remainder of the leaf stem to the stem wire with green floral tape. (Photo 1)

## Beading the Handle

1. Wrap the handle with coordinating floral tape. (Photo 2)

2. Estimate the amount of seed beads needed to wrap the handle by measuring the length of the handle and multiplying the inches by 9. To estimate the number of inches of wire, add 2'–3' (feet) to the length of beads. String size 11° seed beads onto the 28-gauge wire.

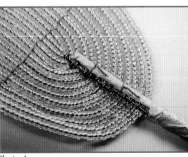

Photo 1

Photo 2

Photo 3

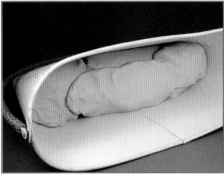
Photo 4

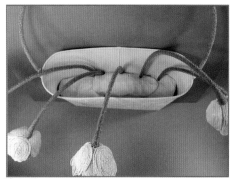
Photo 5

3. Start wrapping the beads at one end of the handle. Wrap a little bare wire around the handle to get started. Keep the beads taut as you wrap. Wrap the entire length of the handle the same way that you wrapped the stems of the tulips. At the end of the handle, wrap a little bare wire around the handle to secure. (Photo 3)

## Assembling the Tulip Tin

1. Fill the tin half full with the nonhardening clay. *Note: It is not necessary to pack the inside of the tin completely full. You can leave some spaces. The clay does not need to be smooth and flat. It simply needs to hold the tulips.* (Photo 4)

2. Insert the five very curved tulips into the clay first. Place them at the tin back so the weight of the tulips will be somewhat balanced as they curve over the sides. (Photo 5)

3. Place the four medium-curved tulips in front of the five tulips. (Photos 6 & 7)

4. Insert the three straighter tulips in front of the four tulips. (Photo 8)

Photo 6

Photo 7

Photo 8

5. Arrange the flowers so they face in different directions.

6. Shape each tulip petal so some petals curve inward and others curve outward. (Photo 9)

7. Add the leaves one at a time in the spaces between the tulips. Place some leaves so that they bend over the tin sides. Place other leaves so that they are right next to the tulip stems. Wrap some leaves around the tulip stems. Make certain the leaf bottoms are below the level of the tin top. (Photo 10)

8. Make certain there is a balanced mixture of the large leaves and the small leaves throughout the arrangement. If necessary, remove a leaf and re-insert it into the clay.

9. When hanging the tulip tin, make certain to use a sturdy hook or door hanger as this piece will be very heavy. (Photo 11)

Photo 9

Photo 10

Photo 11

**TIP**

*Shaping every petal and every leaf is the secret to making tulips that resemble nature.*

# CLAY POT CRITTERS

**What You Need to Know:**
Round Basic on page 18
Pointed Basic on page 22
Beaded Stems on page 45

## Materials (for Wings & Body)

- Size 9° three-cut beads for main wing color (5 strands)
- Size 9° three-cut beads for body & outline wing color (5 strands)
- Size 9° three-cut beads: three different colors (1 Tbsp. of each color)
- 26-gauge colored copper wire to match body color (6 yds)
- 30- or 32-gauge colored copper wire to match body color (1 spool)

## Other Supplies

- 16-gauge stem wire

## Tools

- General Tools on page 12
- Measuring spoons
- Resealable sandwich bag

Photo 1

# Clay Pot Butterfly

## Making the Antennae

1. Cut two 5" lengths from 26-gauge wire. Place one single body-color bead in the center of each wire. Fold the wire in half and twist it together tightly directly underneath the bead so the bead does not float or move on the wire. Twist the entire length of the wire for each antenna. (Photo 1)

2. Hold the two antennae together with the two beads at the top. Leave ¼" of wire beneath the beads and begin twisting the two antennae together. Open the top of the two wires to make a "V." Each wire of the "V" will have one bead on the end. Measure 1¼" from the bottom of the "V." Trim excess wire. (Photo 2)

## Making the Body

1. String 6" of body-color beads on the 26-gauge wire. Wrap these beads around the antennae wires, starting at the bottom of the "V" and continuing to the end. At the end of the body, cut 8" of bare wire off the spool.

2. Insert the bare wire back through the row at the end of the body. Let it come out three rows from the end. Wrap the wire a few times in between the rows of beads on the body to secure. Cut the wire very close to the body. (Photo 3)

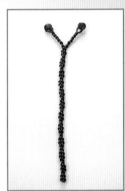

Photo 2

Photo 3

Clay Pot Butterfly  87

Photo 4

Photo 5

Photo 6

Photo 7

Photo 8

When you turn over the first wing to the right side, the two wings will mirror each other.

Photo 9

## Making the Upper Wings

| Pattern: | Make two with the second a mirror image of the first |
|---|---|
| Make 2 | Basic 6, 9 Rows, RBPT |

1. String 12" of main-wing-color beads on the 26-gauge wire. Make the first nine rows, RBPT. To make the tenth row, continue with the main wing color half way up the row. Cut 24" of bare wire from the spool. (Photo 4)

2. Finish the tenth row and the eleventh row with the body color. (Photo 5)

3. Place one tablespoon each of three different-colored beads in a plastic bag and shake. Use mixture of beads to make the next two rows, allowing the colors to mix on the wire at random. (Photo 6)

4. Finish the last two rows with the main body color. Cut the spool wire the length of the loop. Open the loop at the bottom and twist the three wires together. Trim the top basic wire ⅛" from the wing top and bend it to the back. (Photo 7)

5. To make the second wing a mirror image of the first wing, turn the first wing over and copy the colors that you see row by row. (Photo 8)

## Making the Lower Wings

| Pattern: | Make two identical lower wings |
|---|---|
| Make 2 | Basic 6, 7 Rows, RBPT |
| | Leave a 3" top basic wire |

1. String 6" of the main-wing-color beads on the 26-gauge wire. Make the first seven rows RBPT. Measure 18" from the wing bottom and cut the bare wire from the spool.

2. Use the color mixture halfway up the eighth row, followed by the body color to finish the row. Start the ninth row half way with the body color, followed by the bead mixture. (Photo 9)

Photo 10

Photo 11

Photo 12

3. Cut the knot off the top basic wire and add 15 body color beads to the basic wire. Make a new knot. (Photo 10)

4. Add enough of the body color to continue up alongside the wing. Follow the shape of the wing with the extended basic. Make a point at the top and continue down the other side. (Photo 11)

5. Wrap the wire around the bottom basic wire and cut the wire the length of the loop. Open the loop at the bottom and twist the three wires together. Trim the top basic wire 1/8" and bend to the back of the wing. Twist the top half of the wing a couple times from the point where the basic beads were extended. (Photo 12)

## Assembling the Butterfly

1. Place the two upper wings together with the right sides facing each other. Twist the two stem wires together approximately 1". Open the wings, horizontally. Bend the stem wire down. Measure 1/2" from where the two wings join together. Trim excess stem wire. (Photo 13)

Photo 13

2. Attach the two lower wings to each other at the base of the wings. Place the two lower wings together with the right sides facing each other. Twist the two stem wires together approximately 1". Open the wings so they are horizontal. Bend the stem wire up. Measure 1/2" from where the two wings join together and trim excess stem wire. (Photo 14)

### TIP

*Twisting the top half of the wings is an effective way to create tails on your butterfly wings.*

Photo 14

Photo 15

Photo 16

3. Attach the two upper wings to the body with 30- or 32-gauge wire. Place the wings on the bottom of the body and wrap the wire around the stem of the wings and in between the rows of beads on the body. Trim excess wire very close to the body. (Photo 15)

4. Line up the lower wings on the bottom of the body so that the two sets of wings touch or slightly overlap each other. When you have it in the desired place, attach to the body with the 30- or 32-gauge wire by wrapping around the stem of the lower wings and in between the rows of beads on the body. Trim excess wire very close to the body. (Photo 16)

5. Bend the two tails to curve down. (Photo 17)

6. Place a hook in one end of 16-gauge stem wire, using pliers. Cut a piece from the 30- or 32-gauge wire and wrap one end at the hook top where butterfly will be attached. (Photo 18)

7. Attach the butterfly to the stem wire with the 30- or 32-gauge wire. Place the butterfly so that the tail end is at the hook end. Wrap the wire around the stem wire and through the rows of the body to secure. Keep the wire in between the rows so that it will not be visible from the top of the butterfly. Trim stem wire to the desired length. Insert the butterfly into a clay pot. (Photo 19)

Photo 17

Photo 18

Photo 19

# Clay Pot Dragonfly

**What You Need to Know:**
Double Loops on page 55
Beaded Stems on page 45

## Materials (for Wings & Body)

■ Size 9° three-cut beads:
iridescent green (3 strands)
■ 4mm faceted beads: iridescent
green (30)
■ 8mm faceted bead: iridescent
green
■ 24-gauge colored copper wire
in coordinating color (1 yd)
■ 30-gauge colored copper wire
in coordinating color (3 yds)

## Other Supplies

■ 16-gauge stem wire

## Tools

■ General Tools on page 12

## Making the Body & Head

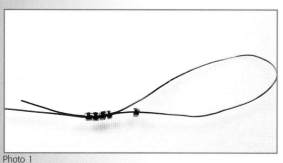
Photo 1

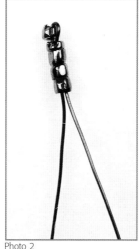
Photo 2

1. Begin with a 12" piece of 30-gauge
wire. String five size 9° three-cut beads
onto the wire and hold beads 3" from
the wire end. Take the 3" wire end and
pass it back all the way through the
beads, skipping the first bead. (Photo 1)

2. Push the beads so they are tight up
against the first bead and do not move.
(Photo 2)

Photo 3

Photo 4

Photo 5

Photo 6

3. Cut the 3" wire close to the beads. (Photo 3)

4. Add enough beads to the other wire end until you have 3" of beads on the wire. This will form the body and the tail. Follow the 3" of beads with the 8mm bead plus one more seed bead. Holding the 8mm bead so that there are no spaces between it and the 3" of seed beads, pass the wire back through the 8mm and pull tightly until all the beads are as tight as possible. (Photo 4)

5. Add 1½" of beads to the wire. (Photo 5)

6. Twist the two strands together until you run out of the 1½" of beads. At this point, wrap bare wire four or five times between two beads on the tail to secure. Trim the wire very close to the beads. (Photo 6)

## Making the Wings

1. On 24-gauge wire, string 22" of size 9° three-cut beads mixed at random with the thirty 4mm faceted beads. For example, start with ½" of seed beads and add a 4mm bead, then add 1" of seed beads and a 4mm bead. Follow this with ¾" of seed beads and another 4mm bead, and so on until all 22" are strung. *Note: It is best to keep the maximum length of seed beads between any two 4mm beads to 1½". This will make all the wings.*

2. Make two large wings. Make a double loop, with the first loop containing 2½" of beads. Leave a 3" tail at the beginning of the loop. Keep the loops long and narrow. *Note: The double loop should have a little space between the loops.* Twist the spool wire and the tail wire for approximately 1" and cut from the spool.

3. Repeat for the second wing. (Photo 7)

4. Place the two wings face to face and twist the stem wires at the base of the wings for 1". Open the wings horizontally.

Photo 7

**NOTE**

*Placing the 4mm beads less than 1½" apart will make it easier to create your dragonfly wings.*

Photo 8

Photo 9

Photo 10

5. Make two small wings. Make a double loop with the first loop containing 1¾" of beads. Leave a 3" tail at the beginning of the loop. Keep the loops long and narrow. *Note: The double loop should have a little space between the loops.* Twist the spool wire and the tail wire for approximately 1" and cut from the spool.

6. Repeat for the second wing. Place the two wings face to face and twist the stem wires at the base of the wings for 1". Open the wings horizontally.

7. Place the smaller wings on top of the larger wings at approximately the center of the larger wings so that they overlap. Use 30-gauge wire to wrap the two stems together for ½" to secure. Using heavy-duty wire cutters, cut the stem to a length of ¾". (Photo 8)

**Assembling the Dragonfly**

1. String 12" of seed beads onto 30-gauge wire. Wrap beads five or six times around the body, beginning beneath the 8mm bead. Do not wrap to the end of the body. (Photo 9)

2. Place the body on top of the wings. Secure the wings to the body with 30-gauge wire. Continue to wrap the beads around the body, making certain to cover the stem of the wings. Stop wrapping at the point where the tail begins. (Photo 10)

3. Push away any excess beads. Wrap bare wire from the same strand between two beads on the tail. Wrap four or five times to secure and cut very close to the body. Use a piece of lacing wire and secure the upper body to the wings just beneath the head, if necessary. (Photo 11)

4. Form a hook in the end of 16-gauge stem wire, using round-nosed pliers. Attach the dragonfly to the stem wire by wrapping a piece of 30-gauge wire around the hook and the dragonfly body. Wrap the 30-gauge wire in between the rows along the body so that the wire does not show. Trim stem wire to desired length and insert into the clay pot. (Photo 12)

Photo 11

Photo 12

# Clay Pot Bumblebee

**What You Need to Know:**
Continuous Loops on page 20
Double Loops on page 55

## Materials (for Body & Wings)

- Size 11° seed beads; or size 9 three-cut beads: black (1 strand)
- Size 11° seed beads; or size 9 three-cut beads: yellow (1 strand)
- 24-gauge colored copper wire: black

## Other Supplies

- 16-gauge stem wire
- Floral tape: green

## Tools

- General Tools on page 12

Photo 1

Due to the lighting variation in the above photograph the bead colors of Clay Pot Bumblebee appear to be different from the step-by-step photographs, but they are not.

## Creating the Bumblebee

1. String 34 black beads onto 24-gauge wire. Make a 7-bead loop, leaving a 3" tail from the loop end. Bend the loop at a right angle to the tail wire. (Photo 1)

Photo 2

Photo 3

Photo 4

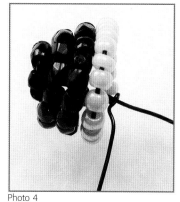

Photo 5

2. Make a 12-bead loop behind the 7-bead loop and twist the wire around the tail wire. Make certain the tail wire remains at a right angle to the loops. (Photo 2)

3. Make a 15-bead loop behind the 12-bead loop and twist the wire around the tail wire. Make certain the tail wire remains at a right angle to the loops. (Photo 3)

4. Cut 12"–15" of bare wire from spool. String enough yellow beads to make a loop slightly larger than the last loop. Since all beads are different sizes, it is not possible to give the exact number of beads for this. Wrap the wire around the tail wire to secure the loop. (Photo 4)

5. String enough black beads to make a loop slightly larger than the last loop. Wrap the wire around the tail wire to secure the loop. (Photo 5)

6. String enough yellow beads to make a loop slightly larger than the last loop. Wrap the wire around the tail wire to secure the loop. (Photo 6)

7. String enough black beads to make a loop slightly smaller than the last loop. Wrap the wire around the tail wire to secure the loop, then string enough yellow beads to make a loop slightly smaller than the last loop. Wrap the wire around the tail wire to secure the loop. (Photo 7)

8. String 12 black beads and make a loop, wrapping the wire around the tail wire to secure the loop.

9. String six black beads and make a loop, wrapping the wire around the tail wire to secure the loop. Twist the spool wire and the tail wire together at the end of the bee. (Photo 8)

Photo 6

Photo 7

TIP

*As you create the body of the bumblebee, it is easy to flatten out the loops. Use the point of a pencil to reshape the loops into circles.*

Photo 8

Clay Pot Bumblebee   95

Photo 9

Photo 10

Photo 11

10. String 6" of black beads onto 24-gauge wire. Make two continuous double loops with the first loop containing 15 beads. Leave a 3" tail at the beginning of the loop and end of the continuous loops. Cut from the spool. (Photo 9)

11. Twist the two tail wires together all the way to the end. (Photo 10)

12. Angle the stem wire of the wings toward the back of the bee. Insert the wings behind the third black row of the bee and push the stem wire out the back loop of the bee. (Photo 11)

13. Twist the wing wires together with the body wires. (Photo 12)

14. Attach the bee tail to the 16-gauge stem wire, using green floral tape. Cut the stem wire to the desired length and insert into the clay pot. (Photo 13)

Photo 12

Photo 13

# Towel Rack

What You Need to Know:

French Beaded Anemones on page 47

## Materials

- Anemones with variations noted below (5)
- 26-gauge assembly wire: white
- Floral tape: white
- Wooden towel tack with open scrollwork*

## Tools

- General Tools on page 12

*When choosing a shelf or towel rack, look for open holes or scroll-work that will allow you to run the wire through. (Photo 1)*

Photo 1

## Making the Anemones

1. Make five Anemones in coordinating colors as follows:

   **a.** Make two medium leaves and four small leaves.

   **b.** Do not attach the leaves to the flowers.

Photo 2

Photo 3

Photo 4

## Decorating the Towel Rack

1. Lay the flowers out on the table or floor to get an idea of placement on the towel rack. (Photo 2)

2. Start with the flower in the center and work out toward the edges. *Note: I covered all my stems with white floral tape because my towel rack is white and I wanted to see as little of the stems as possible.*

3. Cut the stems to lengths that will allow them to hide behind the woodwork. *Note: I cut my stems to 4" lengths.* Wire the stems in the back by twisting the wire as taut as possible, then trim the wire so that it does not hang off the towel rack. (Photo 3)

4. Attach all five flowers to towel rack. (Photo 4)

5. Attach the two medium leaves next to the center flower and the four small leaves next to the two outside flowers. (Photo 5)

6. Try to keep all the wires short and wherever possible tuck them in so they do not scratch the wall when you hang the towel rack. (Photo 6)

Photo 5

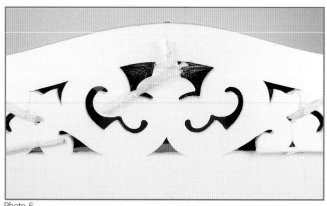
Photo 6

# Lamp Shade

**What You Need to Know:**
French Beaded Hydrangeas on page 53
Beaded Stems on page 45

## Materials (for Lamp Shade)

- Size 10° seed beads; or size 11° seed beads: pink (5 hanks)
- 28-gauge colored copper wire in coordinating color (34 yds)
- Lamp shade frame: 3" x 6" x 4½"

## Materials (for Flowers)

- Size 11° seed beads; or size 9° three-cut beads: light color (2 hanks)
- Size 11° seed beads; or size 9° three-cut beads: dark color (2 hanks)
- Size 6° seed beads in coordinating color for the centers (37)
- 26-gauge colored copper wire in coordinating color (27 yds)

## Tools

- General Tools on page 12

## Beading the Lamp Shade

1. Cut seventeen 72" lengths from 28-gauge wire. Place a knot in the end of each wire and string 54" of beads onto each wire. Place a knot in the other end of each wire.

2. Start at the top ring of the lamp shade. Wrap bare wire around the top ring a few times to get the wrapping started. Wrap the beads around the top ring the same way that you would bead a flower stem. Keep the rows of beads together and keep the beads tight so that no spaces develop along the wire. When you get to the end of the ring, wrap over the wire from the starting end. Wrap bare wire in between the rows of beads a couple times to secure the wire end. Trim the wire close to the beads and tuck the end in between the rows. (Photos 1 & 2)

Photo 1

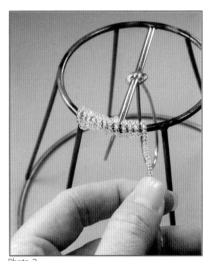
Photo 2

3. Repeat for the bottom ring of the lamp shade. *Note: If you run out of beads on a strand of wire, twist the wire end from the first strand with the beginning of the wire from the new strand. Push the beads together so that they meet with the beads from the old strand. Continue wrapping around the ring. When finished wrapping, go back and wrap the twisted wire at the connection point in between two rows of beads and trim it close to the beads.*

Photo 3

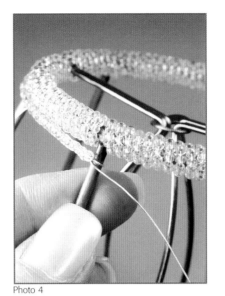

Photo 4

Photo 5

4. Wrap the sides of the lamp shade with beads, beginning at one of the spokes. Always start and end a strand of beads at a spoke. *Note: If you run out of beads and find yourself in between two spokes, end the strand at the last spoke. Do not connect the beads in the middle of the lamp shade. If you did, when you turned on the light, you would see the wire at the connection point.* (Photo 3)

5. Wrap bare wire around the first spoke. Push the beads up to meet the spoke and pull the beads across to the next spoke. Stop the beads at the next spoke and wrap bare wire around that spoke. Wrap from front to back, then around to the front again. (Photo 4)

6. Push the beads up to meet the beads between the spokes. Avoid leaving any spaces. (Photo 5)

7. Continue wrapping the beads around the entire lamp shade. To attach a new strand of beads, end the first strand at a spoke. Twist the first strand and the new strand together for 1". Pull the new strand around the spoke to the front. Push up the beads to meet the beads from the first strand. Continue wrapping. After wrapping around a few more spokes, go back and trim the twisted wire to ¼ and press it flat against the back of the spoke, inside the lamp shade. (Photo 6)

## Making the Flowers

**Pattern: Make 37**

**4 continuous loops:**
**Start with one quadruple loop, followed by one triple loop, followed by one quadruple loop, followed by one triple loop**

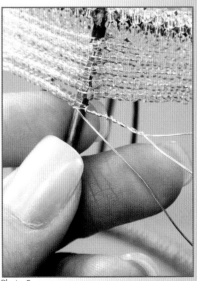

Photo 6

Photo 7

Photo 8

Photo 9

Photo 10

Photo 11

1. Make each flower, following the hydrangea instructions on page 53. Start with 25" of bare wire. Follow the instructions for shading a quadruple or triple loop as necessary. Make the first quadruple loop 3" from the knot in the wire.

2. Start the next triple loop ¼" from the quadruple loop. (Photo 7)

3. Start the next quadruple loop ⅜" from the last triple loop. (Photo 8)

4. Start the last triple loop ¼" from the previous quadruple loop. (Photo 9)

5. Pull one tail wire up to the flower front. Add a size 6° seed bead to the wire. Bring the wire back down to the flower bottom. (Photo 10)

6. Twist the tail wires together to form one stem wire. (Photo 11)

## Decorating the Lamp Shade

1. Attach 13 flowers to the top ring of the lamp shade and 24 flowers to the bottom ring of the lamp shade. Wrap the stem wires of the flower in between the rows of beads around the ring. Trim the wire close to the beads and tuck the ends in between the rows to hide the wire. (Photo 12)

2. Place each flower so the petals of one flower touch the petals of the next flower. (Photo 13)

Photo 12

Photo 13

# Fall Berry Wreath

**What You Need to Know:**
French Beaded Rose Leaves on page 31

## Materials (for Leaves)

- Size 11° seed beads in autumn colors (11 hanks); or size 9° three-cut beads in autumn colors (14 hanks)
- 24- or 26-gauge colored copper wire to match bead color (125 yds)
- 30-gauge colored copper wire to match bead color (34 yds)

## Materials (for Berries) *

- Seed beads left over from leaves (1 bead per berry)
- 4mm–6mm pearl-like beads: autumn colors
- 30-gauge colored copper wire in coordinating color (approximately 86 yards for 384 berries)

## Other Supplies

- 8" dia. brass ring
- 30-gauge paddle wire: green, or 28-gauge assembly wire: silver
- Floral tape: brown

## Tools

- General Tools on page 12

*\* Make as many berries as desired. (There are 780 berries on my wreath.) Decide on the number of berries based on multiples of 48 so that you have the same number of berries for each spray. There will be 48 sprays of leaves. For example, if you want eight berries per spray you would need 384 berries.*

## Making the Leaves

**Pattern: Make 144**

**Basic 4, 13 Rows, RBPT**
**Trim so one long wire extends**
**Lace across each leaf, if desired (Photo 1)**

Photo 1

1. Make one leaf spray, using the following method:

   **a.** Place three leaves on top of each other with the good side facing up. Twist the leaf stems together to make one stem. (Photo 2)

   **b.** Open the leaves to make a fan. (Photo 3)

Photo 2

Photo 3

**c.** Shape the leaves by curving them at the center of each leaf. Set aside until all berries are made. (Photo 4)

2. Repeat for a total of 48 leaf sprays.

Photo 4

## Making the Berries

1. Make desired number of berries, using the following method:

   **a.** Cut 8" piece of 30-gauge wire for each berry. Place one seed bead on the wire. Move the bead to the center and fold the wire in half so the ends are even. Press the wires together. (Photo 5)

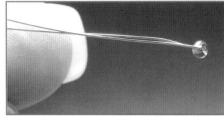
Photo 5

   **b.** Insert the two wire ends through the 4mm bead and push the bead down until it meets the seed bead. Open the wire ends and tie a knot directly beneath the 4mm bead. (Photo 6)

   **c.** Twist the wires together tightly and evenly to form one stem wire. Repeat until all berries are made. (Photo 7)

   **d.** Divide the total number of berries by 48. Make a berry cluster by twisting the stem wires together. Be certain to vary the heights of the stems. Make 48 berry clusters. (Photo 8)

   **e.** Attach one berry cluster to one leaf spray by twisting the stem wires together beneath the leaves to form one stem. *Note: Since the wires can be fairly thick, it is helpful to use nylon-jaw pliers to assist with the twisting of the wires.* Attach the 48 berry clusters to the 48 leaf sprays. (Photo 9)

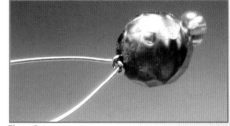
Photo 6

Photo 7

Photo 8

Photo 9

Photo 10

Photo 11

## Assembling the Wreath

1. Tape the brass ring. Be certain to cover the entire ring. (Photo 10)

2. Attach one leaf spray to the ring, using paddle wire or assembly wire. Place the leaf spray directly on top of the ring and center the three leaves along the ring. Tape the stem of the leaves and the ring with enough tape to cover the assembly wire. *Note: If desired, trim the stem wire of the leaves. Trimming the wires has no significant effect on the construction of the wreath, except to make it slightly lighter in weight.* (Photo 11)

3. Attach the next leaf spray to the ring, using paddle or assembly wire. Place this spray ½" below the first spray. Angle the leaves to the left. After wrapping the assembly wire, tape the stem to the ring, covering the assembly wire. (Photo 12)

4. Attach the third spray of leaves to the ring, using paddle wire or assembly wire. Place this spray ½" below the second spray. Angle the leaves to the right. After wrapping the assembly wire, tape the stem to the ring, covering the assembly wire. (Photo 13)

Photo 13

This is the back view of the wreath. Notice that all wires will eventually be covered with floral tape.

Photo 12

Photo 14

*Leaves are spaced adequately by dividing the number of sprays in half or quarters and making certain to fill a quarter or half of the ring with that many sprays. (Photo 14)*

5. Continue adding leaf sprays to the ring at ½" intervals, placing the leaves in the pattern: center, left, right, center, left, right. *Notes: This will ensure that all angles of the wreath are full. The approximate circumference of the ring is 24". Therefore, if leaves are placed at approximately ½" intervals you should have enough to go all the way around.*

6. Continue around the ring until all of the sprays have been added. (Photo 15)

Photo 15

# Wheat Votives

**What You Need to Know:**

4-row Crossover Loop on page 34

## Materials (for one Stalk)

- Size 11° seed beads; or size 9° three-cut beads: light topaz (2 strands)
- 28-gauge colored copper wire: gold (5 yds)

## Materials (for one Votive)

- Size 11° seed beads (5 hanks); or size 9° three-cut beads: light topaz (6 hanks)
- 28-gauge colored copper wire: gold (134 yds)

## Other Supplies

- 6" lengths of 16-gauge stem wire (30)
- 15 oz. packages red rice or other grain for filler (3)
- Floral tape: straw-colored
- Glasses: 2" dia. x 2" tall, 4" dia. x 3½" tall
- Tea-light votive*: 1½" dia. x 2" tall

## Tools

- General Tools on page 12

*You can use many different types of glasses for your votive. You can even use clay pots or other containers that are not see- through.*

> **NOTE**
>
> *This two-tiered votive uses 30 stalks of wheat on short stems to complete the assembly. There are so many different uses for stalks of wheat. Stalks of wheat can be used on long stems, mixed in with other flowers to make an autumn arrangement, or used by themselves, bundled with a ribbon. If you want to make other types of arrangements with the wheat, calculate how much wire and how many beads you will need from the quantities given for making just one stalk.*

## Making the Kernels

**Pattern: Make 40**   **1" 3-row crossover, looping 3" of bare wire over the top**

1. Make each kernel of wheat the same. Leaving a 2" tail, make a single loop with 1" of beads. Press the sides of the loop together to form a narrow loop. (Photo 1)

2. Bring enough beads up the center of the loop as if forming a crossover. Cut 3" of bare wire from the spool. (Photo 2)

3. Loop the bare wire between two beads at the top of the narrow loop of beads. Pull the wire tightly until you hear the wire click in between two of the beads. Straighten the wire at the kernel top. (Photo 3)

Photo 1

Photo 2

Photo 3

Photo 4

Photo 5

4. Assemble the kernels into 20 pairs by twisting two kernels together at the base of the beads. *Note: The kernels will form a "V" shape with one stem wire supporting two kernels. There is a front and back to each kernel. The front is the side with the row of beads crossing up the center of the loop. Keep all the fronts on the same side when forming the pairs.* (Photo 4)

## Assembling the Wheat Votives

1. To make the stalks for the votives, tape a piece of 6" stem wire. Press one pair of kernels together so the front sides face out. Attach this pair of kernels to the top of the stem wire, using half the width of the floral tape. (Photo 5)

2. Attach three pairs of kernels in a circle around the stem wire, placing them so that the tops of these kernels line up with the center of the kernel at the top. Make certain that the fronts face out. (Photo 6)

3. Attach four pairs of kernels around the stem so that the kernel tops line up with the kernel center in the previous row. (Photo 7)

4. Continue attaching the pairs of kernels, four in each row, until all 20 pairs are attached. Continue taping the entire stem length. (Photo 8)

5. Make 30 stalks of wheat for the votive.

Photo 6

Photo 7

Photo 8

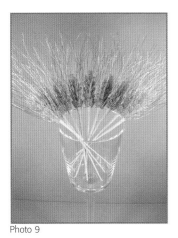

Photo 9

Photo 10

Photo 11

Photo 12

6. In the larger glass container, arrange 16 stalks so they circle the edge of the glass completely. Let the beads of the wheat sit at the edge of the glass. (Photo 9)

7. Carefully fill the glass with the red rice or other grain to hide the stalk stems. Fill with rice up to the edge of the glass. (Photo 10)

8. Arrange 14 stalks in a circle in the smaller glass. (Photo 11)

9. Fill the smaller glass with rice up to the edge. (Photo 12)

10. Place the tea-light votive into the center of the smaller glass. (Photo 13)

11. Place the smaller glass into the center of the larger glass. Be careful not to bend the tops of the wheat stalks. (Photo 14)

**TIP**

*To store your wheat votives, disassemble the votives and wrap each stalk individually in tissue paper, being certain to keep the wire tops straight. Place the wrapped stalks in a shoe box until needed.*

Photo 13

Photo 14

**TIP**

*If the wires of the wheat stalk bend, use nylon-jaw pliers to straighten them out.*

# Mistletoe Ball

What You Need to Know:
Round Basic on page 18
Pointed Basic on page 22

## Materials (for Mistletoe)

- Size 9° three-cut beads: white (1 hank)
- Size 11° seed beads: green (13 hanks); or size 9° three-cut beads: green (15 hanks)
- 26-gauge colored copper wire: green (150 yds)
- 26-gauge colored copper wire in coordinating color (20 yds)

## Materials (for Ball)

- 3" dia. floral Styrofoam ball: green
- 16-gauge stem wire
- Acrylic paint: forest green (2 oz.)
- Assembly wire (6")
- 3"-wide sheer wire-edged ribbon for bow and hanger: white

## Other Supplies

- Floral tape: green

## Tools

- General Tools on page 12
- Drinking glass
- Paintbrush

## Making the Branches

**Patterns: Make 65 branches, with each consisting of three leaves**

> Make 1     **Basic 3, 13 Rows, RTPB, elongate the point Trim so three long wires extend**
>
> Make 2     **Basic 3, 11 Rows, RTPB, elongate the point Trim so three long wires extend**

1. When forming the basic frame to make the leaves, you may shorten the top basic wire, leaving only 1" of wire above the basic beads. Make the bottom loop, using enough wire to twist the bottom stem wire approximately 20 times. *Note: The elongated point will require more wire on the bottom of the leaf than a leaf with a normal point.*

2. To elongate the leaf, make the first four rows so that the bottom is pointed, wrapping the wire so that one bead will sit above the previous row. When making the fifth row, wrap the wire around the basic high enough so that two beads will sit above the previous row. *Note: Leaving two beads instead of one will create a sharper point on the leaf. It will also leave some space inside the leaf. This is OK. Be certain to keep the rows close together at the leaf top and the spaces will not be noticeable when the leaves are assembled into the ball.* (Photo 1)

Photo 1

Photo 2

Photo 3

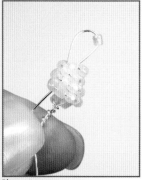

Photo 4

Photo 5

## Making the Berries

**NOTE**

*These berries were adapted from an original design by Estelle Johnson. The pattern was adjusted to account for the difference in size that results from using size 9° three-cut beads.*

**Pattern: Make 60**     **Basic 2, 2 Rows, wrap the beads around the rows to make the berry**
**Add one bead to the basic wire and pull through the berry**
**Trim so one long wire extends**

1. String 2½" of beads on the wire. Make the top basic wire 2½" long. With two beads on the basic wire, create the first row making the top round. (Photo 2)

2. Push the remaining beads up to the basic wire. Wrap the beads around the first row and the basic row until reaching the bottom of the basic beads. *Note: You should be able to wrap the beads around the basic at least three times.* (Photo 3)

3. When reaching the bottom of the basic beads, push away any excess beads and twist the spool wire with the bottom basic wire. Trim so one long wire extends.

4. Cut the knot off the top basic wire and add one bead. (Photo 4)

5. Push the basic wire down through the berry top and out the berry bottom. Twist this wire with the stem wire. (Photo 5)

## Assembling the Mistletoe Ball

1. Tape the stems of all the leaves and all the berries with half the thickness of the tape. (Photo 6)

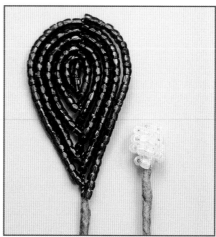

Photo 6

Photo 7

Photo 8

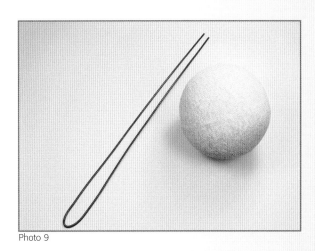

Photo 9

2. Tape two 11-row leaves and one 13-row leaf together, using half the thickness of the floral tape. Place the larger leaf between the two smaller leaves. Leave approximately ¼" of leaf stem showing above the tape that holds the branch together. Using heavy-duty cutters, cut the branch stem to a length of 1". Repeat for all 65 branches. (Photo 7)

3. Tape the berries into clusters of three. Do not trim the stems. (Photo 8)

4. Fold 16-gauge wire in half. (Photo 9)

5. Insert the folded stem wire into the center of the ball. Pull the wire so the fold is at the ball bottom. This will give you a handle to hold the ball as you work. *Note: It will also become the mechanism used to hang the ball when it is finished.* (Photo 10)

6. Paint the ball with forest green paint. Let dry before assembling the mistletoe ball. (Photo 11)

7. Using round-nosed pliers, insert one branch into the ball top. Place it close to the folded stem wire and push until the three separate leaf stems protrude from the ball. *Note: This branch becomes the very bottom of the ball.* (Photo 12)

Photo 10

TIP

*Styrofoam balls are available in white or light green. Even if you purchase a light green ball, paint the ball forest green to hide the spaces between the branches.*

Photo 12

Photo 11

Photo 13

Photo 14

8. Place five more branches circling around the center-bottom branch. Using round-nosed pliers, place the branches accurately and insert all the way into the ball. Place these branches ½" from the center branch and ½" from each other. (Photo 13)

9. Add some berry clusters in between the branches. Let the berry tops peak through the branches. (Photo 14)

10. Continue placing branches in rows circling around the ball. Do not concern yourself with which way the leaves are turning. Randomly place and overlap the leaves to cover as much space as possible on the ball. Place each row ½" from the previous row and each branch ½" from each other. Add berry clusters in between the branches. (Photo 15)

Photo 15

11. Continue adding branches until the ball is three-fourths full. Use a drinking glass to make it easier to work. (Photo 16)

12. Using heavy-duty wire cutters, cut the stem wires so that 1½" of wire is showing at the ball top. (Photo 17)

## TIP

*Placing the mistletoe ball upside down in a large drinking glass rather than setting it down on the table will help prevent the leaves from getting crushed on the bottom.*

Photo 16

Photo 17

13. Using round-nosed pliers, carefully bend the wire ends over each other. Using a small amount of assembly wire, tie the two wires together to form a hook. (Photo 18)

14. Using craft scissors, cut 24" from ribbon. Insert the ribbon through the hook. (Photo 19)

15. Cut a second piece of ribbon to desired length for the hanging the ball. *Note: This piece should be fairly long so that you can tie it together at the top, or make another bow if desired.* (Photo 20)

16. Attach the bow to the top of the hook with a small amount of the assembly wire.

17. Arrange the loops of the bow so they surround the hanger. Trim the ribbon tails to the desired length. (Photo 21)

Photo 18

Photo 19

Photo 20

Photo 21

**TIP**

*Hang the mistletoe ball from a very sturdy hook. This mistletoe ball is fairly heavy and people will be standing under it for the traditional kiss associated with the mistletoe plant.*

# Christmas Tree

**What You Need to Know:**

Continuous Loops on page 20

## Materials (for Beading the Tree)

- Size 11° seed beads*: green (5 hanks)
- 24-gauge colored copper wire: green (60 yds)

## Materials (for Assembling the Tree)

- 7" dia. papier-mâché box: gold
- 16-gauge stem wires (3)
- Floral tape: green
- Industrial-strength multi-purpose adhesive
- Nondrying modeling clay (1 lb.)

## Other Supplies

- Miniature packages or toys
- Star tree top
- Strand of 20 miniature lights
- Tree decorations
- Tree skirt

## Tools

- General Tools on page 12
- Resealable sandwich bags (12)

*This Christmas Tree is traditionally made with green seed beads. However, try using silver seed beads, silver wire, and white floral tape for a different affect. If choosing gold seed beads, coordinate the wire in gold and use brown floral tape.*

## Making the Tree Layers

> **NOTE**
>
> The Christmas Tree is made in a series of layers. There are 11 layers to the tree. All the branches are made in the same manner. The number of inches of beads required to make one branch has been given for each layer so that you can judge if you have enough beads on the wire to make that size branch. All loops on every branch consist of 16 beads. There are six beads between each loop.

**Patterns for Tree Layers:**

| | |
|---|---|
| **Layer 1: 3 loops** | Make 4 branches; one branch requires 3½" of beads |
| **Layer 2: 5 loops** | Make 4 branches; one branch requires 6" of beads |
| **Layer 3: 7 loops** | Make 4 branches; one branch requires 8½" of beads |
| **Layer 4: 9 loops** | Make 4 branches; one branch requires 11" of beads |
| **Layer 5: 11 loops** | Make 5 branches; one branch requires 13½" of beads |
| **Layer 6: 13 loops** | Make 5 branches; one branch requires 16" of beads |
| **Layer 7: 13 loops** | Make 6 branches; one branch requires 16" of beads |
| **Layer 8: 15 loops** | Make 6 branches; one branch requires 18½" of beads |
| **Layer 9: 17 loops** | Make 6 branches; one branch requires 21" of beads |
| **Layer 10A: 15 loops** | Make 4 branches; one branch requires 18½" of beads |
| **Layer 10B: 17 loops** | Make 4 branches; one branch requires 21" of beads |
| **Layer 11A: 19 loops** | Make 4 branches; one branch requires 23½" of beads |
| **Layer 11B: 21 loops** | Make 4 branches; one branch requires 26" of beads |

Photo 1

Photo 2

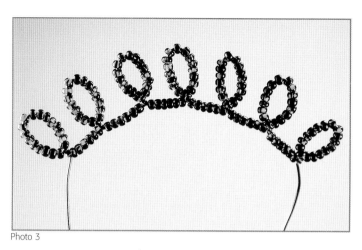

Photo 3

Photo 4

Photo 5

Photo 6

1. Leave approximately 2" of wire before the first loop. Make a loop with 16 beads. Press the sides of the loop together to make it an oval rather than a circle. *Note: The photo below shows the loop before pressing the sides together.* (Photo 1)

2. There are six beads between every loop. Every loop is made of 16 beads. Therefore, push 22 beads up to the first loop. Make the second loop, leaving six beads between the two loops. Press the sides of the loop together to make an oval. (Photo 2)

3. Continue making the required number of loops in each layer. After all the loops have been made, leave 2" of wire and cut from the spool. (Photo 3)

4. Fold the series of loops in half and twist the two end wires together directly underneath the beads. *Note: There will be one loop at the top and pairs of matching loops along the sides.* (Photo 4)

5. Twist the beaded wires between each loop including the top loop. Flatten out the branch. (Photo 5)

6. Angle all the loops in the branch toward the top loop. *Note: This will help to make it look like needles on a branch.* (Photo 6)

7. Place the branches for each layer in a separate resealable bag. Label each bag with the layer number.

Photo 7

Photo 8

Photo 9

Photo 10

Photo 11

Photo 12

Photo 13

## Assembling the Christmas Tree

1. Wrap each 16-gauge stem wire with floral tape. Cut each stem wire to 11". Place the three wrapped wires together and wrap again with floral tape to form the tree trunk.

2. Attach a star treetop ornament to the top of the tree trunk. To make a natural tree, with no decorations or no star, attach one branch from Layer 1 to the top of the stem wire. If you prefer to have a star or other ornament on the top, discard one branch and replace it with the star or ornament. (Photo 7)

3. Bend the remaining branches from Layer 1, one at a time at a right angle to the stem, then place the stem flat against the very end of tree trunk and tape to secure. Circle the branches around the trunk of the tree. (Photo 8)

4. From the top view, the three branches will form a triangle. (Photo 9)

5. Attach the branches of Layer 2. Leave approximately ¼" between the first and second layer. Add the branches one at a time, circling around the tree trunk. (Photo 10)

6. Attach the branches of Layer 3. Leave approximately ¼" between the second and third layer. Add the branches one at a time, circling around the tree trunk. *Note: Try to place the branches in the spaces created by the layer above it. This will create a well-rounded tree.* (Photo 11)

7. Attach the branches of Layer 4. Leave approximately ⅜" between the third and fourth layer. Add the branches one at a time, circling around the tree trunk. *Note: The tree trunk will become thicker as you descend down the tree. This is what you want to happen, as tree trunks do get thicker at the bottom.* (Photo 12)

8. Attach Layers 5 through 9 in the same manner. Leave approximately ½" between each layer. Add the branches one at a time, circling around the tree trunk. (Photo 13)

Photo 15

Photo 16

Photo 17

9. Layers 10 and 11 consist of two different-sized branches in each layer. Alternate Branch A and Branch B within each layer. *Note: The staggered sizes will make the tree look more natural.*

10. Set aside the assembled tree and prepare the tree base.

## Preparing the Tree Base

> **NOTE**
>
> *The base of the tree may be made of any material. However, because the tree is fairly heavy, the base should be deep enough to contain approximately one pound of clay. The clay will support the tree. If you do not plan on putting any toys or decorations under the tree consider potting the tree in an open container.*

Photo 14

1. If using a box with a lid, cut a hole in the top of the box large enough to fit the trunk. Adhere the floral clay to the bottom of the prepared box with adhesive. (Photo 14)

2. Insert the trunk through the hole and push the trunk into the floral clay.

3. Let the adhesive dry overnight before beginning to decorate the tree. (Photo 15)

### Decorating Tips:

■ If placing miniature lights on the tree, I recommend you do this before decorating the branches of the tree in order to conceal the wires of the lights. Wrap the battery pack of the lights and include it as a present under the tree. Cut a small hole in the wrapping paper for the switch and it will be easy to turn the lights on and off. When it is time to change the batteries, simply unwrap the present, replace the batteries, and rewrap the box.

■ Make or purchase decorations for the tree. There are many different kinds of miniature ornaments on the market. Try to purchase ornaments that are less than ½". Anything larger will be out of proportion to the tree. (Photo 16)

■ Use beads as ornaments. Use single large beads. Make seed bead candy canes.

■ Make seed-bead or bugle-bead candles. Larger beads can be used as Christmas balls and seed beads can be strung as garland.

■ Decorate under the tree. Make and wrap miniature presents or purchase ready-made presents. Embellish with toys, rocking horses, sleds, trains, etc. (Photo 17)

■ Remember beaded Christmas trees look lovely without any decorations.

# Glossary

**4-row crossover loop**—A three-dimensional loop containing two interlocking loops where the wire of the second loop crosses over the top of the first loop, and continues down the other side to give the appearance of four rows. 4-row crossover loops may also be continuous.

**Bare wire**—A length of colored copper wire, attached to a petal or leaf, that has been cut from the spool and contains no beads. The beads are added as needed, row by row, to complete the petal or leaf.

**Basic beads**—The number of beads that are placed on the basic wire to start a petal or leaf. It is identified in a pattern as the word "Basic" followed by a number.

**Basic framework**—Made of wire from the spool, it is the structure upon which leaves and petals are created.

**Basic wire**—The top portion of the basic framework. It becomes the center wire of each petal or leaf and contains the basic beads.

**Beaded stems**—The stems of flowers that have beads wrapped completely around the stem, starting immediately beneath the flower and continuing down the length of the stem, stopping a few inches from the bottom of the stem.

**Beehive basic**—The technique used to create a dome shape. Usually used for the centers of flowers.

**Continuous loops**—A series of loops made on one wire. Unless directed otherwise, continuous loops are made so that after the first loop, each subsequent loop is started ⅛" from the previous loop.

**Double loops**—A loop containing two rows of beads, which circle each other where each row is individually twisted to secure. Double loops may also be continuous.

**Elongated point**—A very sharply pointed petal or leaf, achieved by leaving enough space when wrapping the spool wire at a 45-degree angle above a row so that two beads will sit higher than the previous row.

**Lace-as-you-go**—The technique of "sewing" the rows together at the same time that you create each row of the petal or leaf.

**Lacing**—The technique of "sewing" the rows of a petal or leaf together with very fine wire so that the rows will not separate. Usually done after the petal or leaf is created unless you use the Lace-as-you-go method.

**Lacing wire**—Any 30- or 32-gauge colored copper wire used to "sew" the rows of a petal or leaf together.

**Loopback technique**—The technique used to create petals or leaves that contain a central portion that is made on a basic framework, surrounded by loops which protrude from both sides of the petal or leaf. Used to give a frilly or jagged edge appearance.

**Pointed basic**—The technique of making a petal or leaf on a basic framework where the wire is wrapped at a 45-degree angle around the top basic wire or the stem wire to create a pointed shape.

**PTPB**—An abbreviation for the instructions to make a petal or leaf which contains a pointed top and pointed bottom. May also be written as PBPT.

**PTRB**—An abbreviation for the instructions to make a petal or leaf that contains a pointed top and round bottom. May also be written as RBPT.

**Quadruple loop**—A loop containing four rows of beads, which circle each other where each row is individually twisted to secure. Quadruple loops may also be continuous.

**Reverse wrap**—The technique of wrapping the spool wire around the basic wire or stem wire of the basic framework by first bringing the wire behind the basic wire or stem wire before completing a 90-degree or 45-degree wrap.

**Round basic**—The technique of making a petal or leaf on a basic framework where the wire is wrapped at a 90-degree angle around the top basic wire or the stem wire to create a round shape.

**RTPB**—An abbreviation for the instructions to make a petal or leaf that contains a round top and pointed bottom. May also be written as PBRT.

**RTRB**—An abbreviation for the instructions to make a petal or leaf which contains a round top and round bottom. May also be written as RBRT.

**Scalloped edges**—The technique used to create a petal or leaf that has ruffled or serrated edges. It is accomplished by starting the petal or leaf with a basic framework, working from the spool wire, and requires that after a certain number of rows, you cut a specified length of bare wire from the spool. Beads are then added to this bare wire and the rows are worked from side to side to complete the petal or leaf.

**Spool wire**—Colored copper wire that has been prestrung with beads used to create the petals and leaves. Unless specifically directed, the wire should not be cut from the spool while creating the petal or leaf.

**Stem**—The loop end of the basic framework that becomes the wire that supports a petal or leaf. It may also refer to the wire that supports the entire flower.

**Stem wire**—When used in the context of the assembly of a flower, it refers to florists' heavy-gauge wire, sold in straight lengths, which becomes the stem of the entire flower.

**Tail wire**—The amount of wire that is left at the beginning, or end, of a loop or series of loops.

**Triple loop**—A loop containing three rows of beads, which circle each other where each row is individually twisted to secure. Triple loops may also be continuous.

**Donna DeAngelis Dickt** learned the art of French beaded flowers as a child, and has been teaching professionally for the past six years. In addition to conducting workshops and seminars, she is the author of numerous instruction manuals on the subject. Her work can also be seen in *500 Beaded Objects*, *New Dimensions in Contemporary Beadwork*, and *The Portable Crafter: Beading*. Donna lives with her two children Melissa and Ryan, and her husband Larry, in Oak Hill, Virginia.

## Dedication

In loving memory of my father Domenic, who taught me at an early age, "There's nothing we can't learn from a good book."

## Acknowledgments

A special thanks to all the wonderful people at Chapelle, who worked so hard to make a dream of mine come true. To Cindy, thank-you for keeping me calm in the face of my panic attacks, and for sending Rebecca and Vince to me so that I wouldn't need to ship my pieces across the country. I am so grateful. To Karmen, thank-you for putting up with all my computer inadequacies, for making all the parts whole, and for letting me break a rule here and there. It was such a pleasure to work with you. To Rebecca, thank-you for including me, and for creating shots that were better than I could ever have hoped for. You have a wonderful eye. To Vince, thank-you for the lighting tips. In the future, I'll call you when I need an expert. Thanks for making me look so good.

To Michael McCrossin at The Grapevine — Home and Garden Accessories, in Frederick, MD, thank-you for allowing us to come into your store to photograph. Your beautiful home accessories were the perfect complement.

To Jutta and George Terrell at McCleery's Flat, Bed and Breakfast, in Frederick, MD, thank-you for graciously inviting us into your spectacular home to photograph. I know it was hard to see the Forsythia Urn taken down off the mantel. If I ever get the time to make another, I promise I'll call you.

To Terri Gable at Studio Baboo, thank-you for your very generous donations of beads and wire for the forsythia and tulips, and for giving me the opportunity to share my passion with so many incredible ladies, month after month, at our flower classes.

This book would not have been possible without the help of many friends who put in an enormous number of hours beading so that I could bring to life the projects you see on the previous pages. I am forever grateful to you all. I truly could not have done this without you.

To Nicole Krakora, Dianne O'Keefe, and Judy Yiu, the roses in the topiary are stunning. Thank-you.

To Caron Mayo, your original Bistro Pig was darling. Thank-you for letting me share him.

To Nicole Krakora, Caron Mayo, Bron Molloy, Susan Molloy, Joan Rough, Jean Roystone, and Ann Salamini, your excellent work on the forsythia helped to create a masterpiece. Thank-you.

To Judy Yiu, your work is exceptional. The tulips are exquisite. Thank-you.

To Merren Booth, Dianne Carlivati, and Giselle Morris, through all the wheat project transformations, I can't believe you are all still speaking to me. The wheat stalks are magnificent. Thank-you.

To Vicki Purtle, your mistletoe ball is so beautiful, I may hang it up year-round. Thank-you.

To Estelle Johnson, for all your support over the years and for sharing your berry pattern with us, thank-you.

To Dianne Carlivati, for your tireless efforts creating yet another wonderful Christmas tree, thank-you.

Nikki, I owe you a very special note of thanks. You saved me. Your kindness and generosity was overwhelming. You made me laugh, when I wanted to cry. You are an outstanding bead artist and a true friend.

I could not possibly thank my family enough for all that they sacrificed during the writing of this book. Ryan, your meticulous workmanship on the forsythia flowers was amazing. Melissa, I love each and every one of the 250 ornaments you made for the Christmas tree. Thank-you both for being such an inspiration to me. To my husband Larry, who took my place in carpool line, chauffeured the kids to all their activities, did endless loads of laundry, and provided our meals throughout all my beading frenzies, you are my strength. I could not have done this without your support. Thank-you for everything. I love you.

This Bistro Pig is holding french beaded daisies. See page 34.

# Metric Equivalency Charts

mm-millimetres    cm-centimetres
inches to millimetres and centimetres

| inches | mm | cm | inches | cm | inches | cm |
|---|---|---|---|---|---|---|
| 1/8 | 3 | 0.3 | 9 | 22.9 | 30 | 76.2 |
| 1/4 | 6 | 0.6 | 10 | 25.4 | 31 | 78.7 |
| 3/8 | 10 | 1.0 | 11 | 27.9 | 32 | 81.3 |
| 1/2 | 13 | 1.3 | 12 | 30.5 | 33 | 83.8 |
| 5/8 | 16 | 1.6 | 13 | 33.0 | 34 | 86.4 |
| 3/4 | 19 | 1.9 | 14 | 35.6 | 35 | 88.9 |
| 7/8 | 22 | 2.2 | 15 | 38.1 | 36 | 91.4 |
| 1 | 25 | 2.5 | 16 | 40.6 | 37 | 94.0 |
| 1 1/4 | 32 | 3.2 | 17 | 43.2 | 38 | 96.5 |
| 1 1/2 | 38 | 3.8 | 18 | 45.7 | 39 | 99.1 |
| 1 3/4 | 44 | 4.4 | 19 | 48.3 | 40 | 101.6 |
| 2 | 51 | 5.1 | 20 | 50.8 | 41 | 104.1 |
| 2 1/2 | 64 | 6.4 | 21 | 53.3 | 42 | 106.7 |
| 3 | 76 | 7.6 | 22 | 55.9 | 43 | 109.2 |
| 3 1/2 | 89 | 8.9 | 23 | 58.4 | 44 | 111.8 |
| 4 | 102 | 10.2 | 24 | 61.0 | 45 | 114.3 |
| 4 1/2 | 114 | 11.4 | 25 | 63.5 | 46 | 116.8 |
| 5 | 127 | 12.7 | 26 | 66.0 | 47 | 119.4 |
| 6 | 152 | 15.2 | 27 | 68.6 | 48 | 121.9 |
| 7 | 178 | 17.8 | 28 | 71.1 | 49 | 124.5 |
| 8 | 203 | 20.3 | 29 | 73.7 | 50 | 127.0 |

## yards to metres

| yards | metres | yards | metres | yards | metres | yards | metres | yards | metres |
|---|---|---|---|---|---|---|---|---|---|
| 1/8 | 0.11 | 2 1/8 | 1.94 | 4 1/8 | 3.77 | 6 1/8 | 5.60 | 8 1/8 | 7.43 |
| 1/4 | 0.23 | 2 1/4 | 2.06 | 4 1/4 | 3.89 | 6 1/4 | 5.72 | 8 1/4 | 7.54 |
| 3/8 | 0.34 | 2 3/8 | 2.17 | 4 3/8 | 4.00 | 6 3/8 | 5.83 | 8 3/8 | 7.66 |
| 1/2 | 0.46 | 2 1/2 | 2.29 | 4 1/2 | 4.11 | 6 1/2 | 5.94 | 8 1/2 | 7.77 |
| 5/8 | 0.57 | 2 5/8 | 2.40 | 4 5/8 | 4.23 | 6 5/8 | 6.06 | 8 5/8 | 7.89 |
| 3/4 | 0.69 | 2 3/4 | 2.51 | 4 3/4 | 4.34 | 6 3/4 | 6.17 | 8 3/4 | 8.00 |
| 7/8 | 0.80 | 2 7/8 | 2.63 | 4 7/8 | 4.46 | 6 7/8 | 6.29 | 8 7/8 | 8.12 |
| 1 | 0.91 | 3 | 2.74 | 5 | 4.57 | 7 | 6.40 | 9 | 8.23 |
| 1 1/8 | 1.03 | 3 1/8 | 2.86 | 5 1/8 | 4.69 | 7 1/8 | 6.52 | 9 1/8 | 8.34 |
| 1 1/4 | 1.14 | 3 1/4 | 2.97 | 5 1/4 | 4.80 | 7 1/4 | 6.63 | 9 1/4 | 8.46 |
| 1 3/8 | 1.26 | 3 3/8 | 3.09 | 5 3/8 | 4.91 | 7 3/8 | 6.74 | 9 3/8 | 8.57 |
| 1 1/2 | 1.37 | 3 1/2 | 3.20 | 5 1/2 | 5.03 | 7 1/2 | 6.86 | 9 1/2 | 8.69 |
| 1 5/8 | 1.49 | 3 5/8 | 3.31 | 5 5/8 | 5.14 | 7 5/8 | 6.97 | 9 5/8 | 8.80 |
| 1 3/4 | 1.60 | 3 3/4 | 3.43 | 5 3/4 | 5.26 | 7 3/4 | 7.09 | 9 3/4 | 8.92 |
| 1 7/8 | 1.71 | 3 7/8 | 3.54 | 5 7/8 | 5.37 | 7 7/8 | 7.20 | 9 7/8 | 9.03 |

# INDEX